D1561297

Jack

KEROUAC

Alison M. Behnke

Twenty-First Century Books
Minneapolis

For Jack

Copyright © 2007 by Lerner Publications Company

Twenty-First Century Books
A division of Lerner Publishing Group
241 First Avenue North
Minneapolis, MN 55401 U.S.A.

Website addresses: www.lernerbooks.com
                   www.biography.com

Library of Congress Cataloging-in-Publication Data

Behnke, Alison.
    Jack Kerouac / by Alison M. Behnke.
      p.   cm. — (Biographies)
    Includes bibliographical references and index.
    ISBN-13: 978-0-8225-6614-4 (lib. bdg. : alk. paper)
    ISBN-10: 0-8225-6614-1 (lib. bdg. : alk. paper)
    1. Kerouac, Jack, 1922–1969—Juvenile literature. 2. Authors, American—20th century—Biography—Juvenile literature. 3. Beat generation—Biography—Juvenile literature. I. Title. II. Series: A&E biography (Twenty-First Century Books (Firm))
    PS3521.E735Z575 2007
    813'.54—dc22 [B]   2006016516

Manufactured in the United States of America
1 2 3 4 5 6 – BP – 12 11 10 09 08 07

CONTENTS

Jack Kerouac walking in New York City in 1953. Kerouac's
friend and fellow author Allen Ginsberg took this photo.

INTRODUCTION

> The only people for me are the mad ones, the
> ones who are mad to live, mad to talk, mad to be
> saved, desirous of everything at the same time,
> the ones who never yawn or say a commonplace
> thing, but burn, burn, burn like fabulous yellow
> roman candles.
>
> —Jack Kerouac, *On the Road*

On a summer day in 1947, Jack Kerouac stood at the
side of the road in Gothenburg, Nebraska, trying to hitch
a ride. He found one, hopping on "a truck, with a flat-
board at the back, with about six or seven boys sprawled
out on it, and the drivers, two young blond farmers from
Minnesota, were picking up every single soul they found
on that road." Lying on the back of that truck, under the
open sky, Kerouac swapped stories with a ragtag bunch
of fellow wanderers and watched the country roll by.

In 1947 Jack Kerouac was twenty-five years old, an
aspiring writer, a college dropout, and a young man
eager for change—big change. Never having explored
much beyond his East Coast home, he itched to see
and understand more of his world and especially his
country. In a time when the United States seemed
bound up by rigid rules and narrow-minded expectations, he wanted to experience life to its fullest. He
wanted adventure and passion.

Neal Cassady (left), pictured here with Kerouac in the late 1940s, urged Kerouac to travel. The two went on many road trips together.

Kerouac's friend Neal Cassady wanted the same thing, and he encouraged Kerouac's urge to travel. Kerouac later wrote that meeting Cassady "began the part of my life you could call my life on the road. Before that I'd often dreamed of going West to see the country, always vaguely planning and never taking off."

When Kerouac finally hit the road, he made up for lost time, traveling thousands of miles in crisscrossing journeys through the United States and beyond. Hitchhiking, busing, and sometimes hopping trains, he loved meeting people in his travels—especially other people who were true to themselves and lived with little regard for society's constraints.

Even greater than Kerouac's passion for travel was his love of writing. He recorded thousands and thousands of words about his experiences. Travel and writing came together in his book *On the Road*, describing some of his journeys. The book became a smash hit in 1957. Kerouac himself became one of the most important figures of the so-called Beat Generation, a loose group of young writers, artists, wanderers, and thinkers. He would even be called King of the Beats— a title he wore uneasily. In truth, Jack Kerouac was a shy man who delighted in life's small pleasures. But his bigger dreams—his constant pursuit of "joy, kicks, darkness, music"—spoke to a generation.

A smokestack towers over Jack Kerouac's hometown of Lowell, Massachusetts, in the early 1940s. The city's many textile mills were the foundation of its economy.

Chapter **ONE**

LOWELL DAYS

THE BROWN BUILDING WASN'T MUCH TO LOOK AT. None of the houses in this part of Lowell were anything fancy. It was a neighborhood of working people, in a town of working people.

But on March 12, 1922, happiness filled the second-floor apartment at 9 Lupine Road, Lowell, Massachusetts. That evening a baby boy was born to Leo-Alcide Kerouac and Gabrielle-Ange Lévesque Kerouac. The French Canadian couple named their son Jean-Louis Lebris de Kerouac. For short, they called him Jack or Ti Jean—an affectionate name meaning "Little John."

Jack was the Kerouacs' third child. Their little girl, Caroline (nicknamed Nin), was three and a half years old. Jack's older brother, Gerard, was five and a half. Leo and

Gabrielle were immigrants from Quebec, the French-speaking province of Canada. Their ancestors had been immigrants too, traveling across the ocean from France to Canada in the eighteenth century. Starting in the 1840s, many thousands of Quebecers left home and streamed into New England looking for work. Some, including the Kerouacs, ended up in Lowell.

In the mid-nineteenth century, Lowell had been a thriving center of the textile industry. The Merrimack and Concord rivers powered bustling fabric mills that employed thousands of workers. The town prospered, and its population swelled, largely with immigrants. Jack would later describe his hometown, writing of "the textile factories built in brick, primly towered, solid . . . ranged along the river and the canals, and all night the industries hum and shuttle."

But in the late 1800s, new machines replaced workers. Thousands of people lost their jobs. Even so, mill owners did not add machines quickly enough, and Lowell's factories grew more and more outdated. By the time Ti Jean arrived, hard times had hurt the once-flourishing town. Dozens of mills and other businesses had closed.

Fortunately for the Kerouacs, their livelihood did not depend on the mills. Leo worked as a printer and owned his own successful shop, Spotlight Print, in downtown Lowell. He made advertising flyers for other local businesses and published a small newspaper.

Jack's mother, Gabrielle, was a tireless homemaker. Jack and his siblings called her Mémêre, a French term of affection, literally meaning "old lady." Tending to her family's needs, she prepared hearty meals of pork chops, potatoes, stew, and beans, often serving pie or cake for dessert. Jack loved his mother's cooking and wrote warmly of a family meal: "My father comes home from his printing shop and undoes his tie and removes [his] 1920's vest and sits himself down at hamburger and boiled potatoes and bread and butter... with the kiddies and the good wife."

Like many French Canadians, Mémêre was deeply religious. She faithfully attended Mass (Catholic church service) every Sunday and took her children with her. The sensations of Catholic worship embedded themselves in Jack's memory. Many years later, he wrote vividly of a Christmas Mass: "From the open door of the church warm and golden light swarmed out on the snow. The sound of the organ and singing could be heard. Inside ... the delightful smell of overcoats fresh from the cold night mingled with the incense and flowers. Everyone was settling down for Mass, the men ... looking around and nodding, the women adjusting their hats and prayer-beads with sharp prim movements."

"SAINTLY GERARD"

One of the most important people in Jack's earliest years was his brother. Gerard was a sensitive child, a devoted Catholic, and the pride of his mother's heart. He also had a soft spot for animals, and his beloved pet cats scampered through the Kerouac home. Jack remembered Gerard as the one "who warned me to be kind to little animals and took me by the hand on forgotten little walks."

But Gerard developed rheumatic fever, a disease causing inflammation around the heart. He was frail and often ill. When he and Jack were playmates, it was often only Jack who played, while Gerard lay in bed. The family worried and fussed over their sick child as he suffered painfully swollen legs and other symptoms of his illness.

Then, in July 1926, Gerard fell more seriously ill than ever before. He ailed in bed for days, feverish and weak. On July 26, at the age of nine, he died.

The Kerouac family was devastated. Four-year-old Ti Jean was not only saddened but also badly frightened by his big brother's death. Terrified of sleeping alone, he would crawl into Mémère's bed for comfort and safety.

Plunged into grief, Mémère turned to her religion. She found some peace when Gerard's teachers at the Catholic school suggested that the unusually kind and religious boy might have been a young saint—a holy spirit on Earth. Much later, Jack would write about his brother in a way that was part memory and part myth. He described "Saintly Gerard, his pure and tranquil face, the mournful look of him, the piteousness of his little soft shroud of hair falling down his brow and swept aside by the hand over blue serious eyes."

Gabrielle's remaining children brought her some comfort. She doted on Jack especially, and the mother

WRITE WHAT YOU KNOW

hen Jack Kerouac wrote the novels that would eventually make him famous, he drew very heavily on his own life. In fact, his books are so autobiographical that they fall somewhere between fact and fiction. As he wrote in one novel, "Memory and dream are intermixed in this mad universe."

Most of the characters in Kerouac's books can be matched up with people in his life. His family was usually called by the name Duluoz, with himself as Jack Duluoz, his father as Emil Duluoz, and so forth. Kerouac called the books that followed this pattern the Duluoz Legend, which he described as "a lifetime of writing about what I'd seen with my own eyes, told in my own words . . . a contemporary history record for future times to see what really happened and what people really thought."

Although Kerouac's words reflect his life and memories, it's sometimes difficult to know when he exaggerated or misremembered things. He was, after all, an author of novels, and he fictionalized some events to make his books more interesting or artistically pleasing. Nevertheless, readers can learn a lot about Kerouac, his life, and his world from these vivid and very personal writings.

and son grew very close. Leo, too, mourned his lost child. But while his wife turned to church and family, Leo sought relief through spending time with friends at neighborhood bars. He was also fond of gambling, especially playing poker and betting on horse races. By 1927 the family had run into money troubles.

Gabrielle found a job at a local shoe factory to boost the household's income. But just two years later, times grew harder with the onset of the Great Depression (a severe downturn in the national economy). From then on, the Kerouacs lived on a tighter budget than ever.

GROWING

Even with the terrible shadow that Gerard's death cast over Jack's young life, he found some magic in the streets and wildernesses of his hometown. He spent a lot of time on his own, exploring neighborhoods and "roam[ing] fields and riverbanks day and night."

Jack began school when he was about six years old. He attended a Catholic elementary school where the teachers were nuns. At home, Jack had spoken only French, the language of his parents. In school he learned English. He struggled with the new language at first but over time came to love its richness and variety.

When Jack was about ten, his family settled in Lowell's Pawtucketville neighborhood, made up mostly of other French Canadian families. Jack played baseball and football with fellow Pawtucketville kids. The summer he was thirteen, he took up running—even building his own timing device to clock himself and others as they raced on a run-down track. Jack enjoyed the challenge of running and spent hours pushing himself to go faster and faster. He later wrote of "great gloomy track meets in Textile field at sunset with the last event after dark."

Sports were not Jack's only pastime. He loved to

read—especially the fiction-filled magazines that Lowell newsstands sold for a dime each. His favorite character was the Shadow, a suave hero who fought crime and evildoing on dark city streets. In addition to magazine stories, the Shadow was also the subject of a popular radio show. The line that opened each episode was "Who knows what evil lurks in the hearts of men? The Shadow knows!"

Jack had a rich and active imagination. He frequently jotted down ideas and bits of stories in cheap notebooks. He created comic strips, magazines, and even "wrote little novels in my room, first novel written at age 11."

UPS AND DOWNS

In March 1936, when Jack was fourteen years old, the Merrimack River flooded its banks after heavy winter rains. The floodwaters invaded Leo Kerouac's shop, forcing him to close the business. In despair and worry, Leo drank more often and more heavily. He and Gabrielle argued frequently.

Meanwhile, Jack was growing into a young man. He had visions of becoming a professional writer, even discussing the idea with a priest. He also continued to pursue sports, competing in track and playing as a halfback on the Lowell High School football team. He was not especially tall, but he was solidly built and muscular. And he was handsome, with a thick head of dark hair and shining blue eyes.

Jack looks tough in his Lowell High School football uniform. Jack's skill as a player caught the attention of coaches at two colleges.

Around this period, Jack fell in with a new group of friends, four boys with whom he played cards, talked about girls and sports and the future, and generally goofed around. Soon he also had a girlfriend, Mary Carney, whom he met at a New Year's Eve dance. Their first meeting was not exactly smooth. Years later, Jack described a similar scene in his novel *Maggie Cassidy*, based on his romance with Mary. He said, "I put my hard arm around her soft waist and took her dancing awkward dumb steps under the balloons and crinkly pop funhats of New Year's Eve America." Following this fumbling start, the teenagers fell in love and even talked about marrying someday.

By 1939, his senior year, Jack had emerged as one of the brightest stars of the football team. At the big Thanksgiving game, against one of Lowell High

School's fiercest rivals, Jack scored the winning touchdown. His exceptional performance that year would turn out to be a big break. His family could not afford to send him to a good college without help. But before long, both Boston College and New York City's Columbia University offered him football scholarships. With his mother's urging, Jack chose Columbia.

To receive the Columbia scholarship, Jack first had to spend one year at the Horace Mann School for Boys. Located in the New York City borough of the Bronx, Horace Mann was Columbia's preparatory school. This private high school helped students get ready for university-level study. So after graduation from Lowell High in June 1939, Jack packed his bags and said good-bye to his parents, sister, and Mary. He was on his way to the Big Apple—New York City.

Kerouac poses after his graduation from Horace Mann in 1940.

Chapter **TWO**

COLLEGE BLUES AND NEW VIEWS

DURING HIS YEAR AT HORACE MANN, JACK LIVED with a relative in Brooklyn, a borough south of the Bronx. Getting from the Brooklyn apartment to school took two hours or more by subway, but the long commute gave Jack time to observe the citizens of his new home. He wrote, "People are interesting in the subway when you're seventeen and you've never savored the big city. I was a really contented kid to see myself at last among the great mountains of glittering buildings."

At Horace Mann, Jack played on the football team, made up largely of other scholarship students. But many of the boys at Horace Mann were quite wealthy. He described them arriving at school, these "sons of furriers, famous realtors, thissa and thatta and here come mobs of them in big black limousines." Jack stuck out in his modest clothes and old shoes. Nevertheless, he plunged into school life and soon made friends.

Classes and football kept Jack's days full. But he hadn't forgotten about writing. He was a reporter for the *Horace Mann Record*, the school newspaper, and wrote for the school literary magazine, the *Horace Mann Quarterly*. That fall the *Quarterly* printed his short story "The Brothers," a mystery with echoes of Jack's beloved Shadow tales.

Meanwhile, New York City opened up a whole new world to Jack. He loved Lowell, but its dime stores, lunch counters, and quiet streets couldn't compare to the excitement of New York. The metropolis was a bustling, thriving center of business and international affairs, and it was also a creative hub. From poetry and painting to theater and music, every type of art was practiced, shared, and studied.

Jack and his schoolmates sometimes rode into Manhattan, the heart of the city. His close friend Seymour Wyse was a jazz fan, and he took Jack to jazz clubs in Greenwich Village and also in Harlem, the city's main African American neighborhood. In the 1930s and 1940s, it was unusual and even frowned upon for white students to socialize with African American musicians. But Jack fell in love with jazz and its stars, admiring trumpet player Roy Eldridge and saxophonists Charlie Parker and Lester Young—all destined to become legends. Jack described the thrill of entering one of New

Jazz saxophonist Charlie Parker—nicknamed "Bird"—performs in the 1940s. Parker was one of the many jazz artists Kerouac discovered during his time at Horace Mann.

York's clubs: "Outside, in the street, the sudden music which comes from the nitespot fills you with yearning for some intangible joy—and you feel that it can only be found within the smoky confines of the place."

At the end of his year at Horace Mann, Jack headed home to Lowell. Over the summer, he spent a lot of time with his good friend Sebastian Sampas. Sebastian—sometimes called Sammy—introduced Jack to the works of new American authors such as William Saroyan and Thomas Wolfe. Saroyan's loosely structured stories and Wolfe's autobiographical novels deeply influenced Jack's own writing.

Jack also saw Mary Carney that summer. He still cared for her, although he had dated other girls while at Horace Mann. But while they had once discussed marrying, Mary wanted only to stay in Lowell. Jack had bigger dreams—dreams of a life that Lowell could never offer. Jack and Mary would continue to see each other periodically, but talk of marriage seemed to be over. In the autumn of 1940, eighteen-year-old Jack Kerouac left Lowell behind again for his freshman year at Columbia and the bustle of the Big Apple.

CAMPUS LIFE

Columbia's campus stretched through New York City's Morningside Heights neighborhood. The prestigious 186-year-old university was filled with students from all over the United States. Kerouac lived in a dormitory near the heart of the action. Juggling schoolwork and football, he also worked as a dishwasher in the cafeteria to help cover his expenses. And he still found room in his days to explore New York further.

Very soon, however, Kerouac had a lot more time on his hands. In one of the early games of the football season, he was tackled hard and broke his leg. His career as a college sports star came to an abrupt end—at least for that year.

Having come to Columbia with the rather romantic idea of himself as both football hero and budding artist, Kerouac was deeply disappointed. Nevertheless, he made the most of his freshman year. He wrote that he "hobbled every night to the Lion's Den, the Columbia fireplace-and-mahogany-type restaurant, sat right in front of the fire in the place of honor, watched the boys and girls dance, ordered every blessed night the same rare filet mignon . . . then two hot fudge sundaes for dessert, that whole blessed sweet autumn."

When his leg had healed enough, Kerouac continued to prowl the city, read, and talked with friends. And he wrote. He would later recall long nights of composing stories and plays, questioning their merit and his talent, and then writing some more. "I am seated here in my room, at two o'clock in the morning," he wrote. "The page is long, blank, and full of truth. When I am through with it, it shall probably be long, full, and empty with words. . . . I am not trying to copy anyone. I am truthful to myself. I shall write as if I had just been born."

At the end of the school year, Kerouac returned to Lowell. That summer Leo and Gabrielle moved to West Haven, Connecticut, where Leo had found work. Kerouac was sad to see his parents leave his hometown, but he dutifully helped them pack and move.

Kerouac and his sister, Caroline, at home in Lowell. In the summer of 1941, their parents moved to West Haven, Connecticut, and Kerouac wrote to Caroline about how beautiful it was there.

Looking on the bright side, he wrote to his sister (who by then had married and left home) about the gorgeous view in West Haven. He told Caroline, the new place "look[s] smack at the sea. . . . Oh, I tell you, it's *beautiful*. Every time you look out the parlor window you can see the ocean, and sometimes the high tide splash sprays over the sea wall across the street."

In September 1941, back at Columbia, Kerouac looked forward to returning to the football field. But his coach, Lou Little, didn't put him in the starting lineup for the season's first game. Offended and confused, Kerouac abruptly walked off the field—and off campus. Only a few hours later, he was on a bus to Washington, D.C. Kerouac didn't even know what he planned to do next. Yet he was somehow sure that he'd just made "the most important decision of [his] life so far."

Kerouac traveled to Washington dreaming of visiting Virginia and other places he'd read of in Thomas Wolfe's fiction. As it turned out, he was too broke to make the whole trip. Instead, he scraped together bus fare back to Connecticut and his parents. When he got there, Leo and Gabrielle were furious that he'd quit Columbia. Leo insisted that Jack find a job and earn his own money. By October Kerouac was pumping gas at a little station in Hartford, Connecticut. Living on his own in a rented room, he also rented an Underwood typewriter on which he tapped out stories after work. When his parents moved back to Lowell the next month, Kerouac joined them. He found a new job, writing sports articles for the *Lowell Sun* newspaper. But he was restless.

In spring 1942, Kerouac returned to Washington, D.C. He worked on a construction crew in Arlington, Virginia, helping build the U.S. War Department's brand-new Pentagon. The job didn't last long, however, as Kerouac had a tendency to wander off, exploring and dreaming. In a letter to Norma Blickfelt, a young woman he'd dated in New York, he confessed his difficulty staying on task. One day, he said, an African American worker "went by... with his shovel, singing the loveliest blues I ever heard—and I followed him all over the field, listening and smoking." Another time he "hitch-hiked away from the project and spent the afternoon wandering through Virginia fields and villages."

With his final paycheck in hand from that job, Kerouac had enough cash to travel. He went south "with visions of whole afternoons drowsing on a New Orleans river wharf." But a sudden attack of worry about his future and his responsibilities struck him on the way. He decided to try again at Columbia. He headed back to Lowell to make arrangements for returning to school.

HIGH SEAS

By then the United States was fighting in World War II (1939–1945). Kerouac was eager both to defend his country and to see more of the world. He also needed to earn money before he could go back to Columbia.

Joining the military seemed to fill all his needs. Kerouac enlisted in the U.S. Merchant Marine, a fleet of ships carrying troops, weapons, and supplies to the war's European battlegrounds. Boarding the SS *Dorchester*, he shipped out for Greenland in July 1942. He worked as a ship scullion (kitchen helper), scrubbing pots and pans and doing some cooking. He spent his little free time reading and observing ship life, writing to Norma, "What romance!...to stand on a deck bare-chested at dawn, and to listen to the pulse-beats of the ship's great, idle engine."

Kerouac had a brush with death when German submarines attacked the *Dorchester* in the icy waters of the North Atlantic. During the attack, he was frying bacon in the kitchen, listening to the deep booms of the ship's guns. Standing at the range, he began "thinking of that kid on the German submarine who's also makin the bacon. And who is now chokin[g] to death in drowning."

When Kerouac sailed home in October, he learned that Lou Little, the Columbia coach, was ready to have him back on the team. Kerouac returned to school. Once more, however, Little put Kerouac on the bench. And once more, Kerouac walked out and went home to Lowell. He worked odd jobs, read, and began writing a novel called *The Sea Is My Brother*.

Kerouac's time aboard the *Dorchester* had not satisfied his hunger for travel, and he still had dreams of circling the globe with the navy. Writing to Sebastian Sampas, he described visions of "travel to the Mediterranean ports, perhaps Algiers . . . perhaps the old ports of Spain; and Belfast, Glasgow, Manchester . . . Rio and Trinidad . . . and the far-flung Polynesias." In March 1943, Kerouac joined the U.S. Navy. When he flunked the exam to enter the officer training program, he ended up at boot camp in Newport, Rhode Island.

At twenty-one, training with a bunch of younger recruits, Kerouac felt restless and confined. He later claimed, "I didn't mind the eighteen-year-old kids too much but I did mind the idea that I should be disciplined to death." He started disobeying some of the navy's many rules. One day he'd had enough. As he wrote in his book *Vanity of Duluoz,* "I lay my gun down into the dust and just walked away from everybody forever more. I went to the Naval library to read some books and take notes. They came and got me with nets."

Whether that account was literally true or not, Kerouac was promptly placed under observation by navy doctors, who were concerned about his mental health. He spent weeks in the hospital, answering the doctors' detailed personal questions and writing letters home. In May he was honorably discharged from the navy for having a "schizoid personality" and an "indifferent character."

OLD AND NEW FRIENDS

Out of the military, Kerouac went back to living with his parents. They had moved again, renting an apartment on Long Island, not far from New York City. After one more brief stint with the U.S. Merchant Marine in the autumn of 1943, Kerouac settled into the Long Island home for the winter of 1943–1944. He fell into a familiar schedule, working a few jobs but concentrating on reading and writing. He also picked up a relationship he'd begun earlier with a Columbia student named Frankie Edith Parker. Edie, as she was called, was lively, lovely, and wealthy enough to throw a good party. Kerouac described her as having an "eagering grin and laugh." He introduced her to his

Edie Parker began a relationship with Kerouac in 1943. At the time, Kerouac was living with his parents on Long Island and Edie was a student at Columbia. Kerouac would later describe Edie as having "an eagerness entire that . . . endows the lady with the promise that she will look good all her life."

parents, and the couple visited her family in Michigan. In fact, they were nearly inseparable that winter and spring. At Edie's apartment, Kerouac often stayed up writing all night. Edie later recalled, "Every night, no matter how late we were up and out, I went to sleep with a typewriter in my ear."

In March 1944, Kerouac received tragic news: Sebastian Sampas had been killed in the war. When Kerouac learned that his dear friend lay dead in an Italian hospital, he was crushed. He wrote Sebastian a mournful letter, asking, "It's raining—and the song has come—I'll See You Again. Where? Where, Sammy?"

Even as Kerouac grieved for his old friend, he was meeting a host of new ones through Edie. He later remembered that season as a turning point. "Sad nights, rain drumming on the roof, six flights up, on 118th Street and Amsterdam . . . and in start coming the new characters of my future 'life.'"

(Left to right) *Hal Chase, Kerouac, Allen Ginsberg, and William S. Burroughs pose for a photo near Columbia University in the mid-1940s.*

Chapter **THREE**

CAST OF CHARACTERS

THE NEW CHARACTERS IN KEROUAC'S LIFE WERE A colorful bunch. Many, like Kerouac, were aspiring writers. Three major figures were Allen Ginsberg, William Burroughs, and Lucien Carr.

Ginsberg, a Columbia student, had a poet for a father and dreamed of his own literary career. He was interested in new ways of writing and communicating. At eighteen, he was four years younger than Kerouac. Burroughs, in contrast, was eight years older than Kerouac and had already been through college, graduate school, travels in Europe, a marriage, a divorce, and a stint in the army. Carr was a nineteen-year-old Columbia student who happily spent hours discussing literature and the artistic life.

While most Americans of this era focused on traditional goals of marriage, home, and family, these young people openly questioned the value of such conventions. They were driven to discover more about their world and to explore what life offered beyond the conservative boundaries of the time. "The happiest days of my life, I can tell you, were . . . at Columbia when all the kids were around," Kerouac later wrote to his sister. "You'd wake up in the morning and find the house full of people talking or reading books, and you'd go to bed at night with most of them still there. . . . If I had a million bucks, I'd have a mansion . . . and the house would be full of my friends all day long, with concerts going on in the record room."

TUMULTUOUS TIMES

In the summer of 1944, a sudden and violent act disrupted the easy rhythm of those days at Columbia. One hot August night, Carr got into a fight with a friend named David Kammerer—a terrible fight that ended with Carr stabbing Kammerer to death. After throwing the body into the Hudson River, Carr went to Burroughs for advice. Burroughs wisely told Carr to turn himself in to the police. But first Carr headed to Kerouac's place, begging him to go out for a few drinks before he handed himself over to the law. Kerouac—not so wisely—agreed. When Carr was arrested later, Kerouac and Burroughs were also arrested as witnesses.

Thrown into jail and short on cash, Kerouac couldn't pay his bail. His father refused to help, so Kerouac turned to Edie. She agreed to give him the money—and Kerouac agreed to get married. Meanwhile, the authorities dropped the charges against Kerouac, as long as he provided testimony at Carr's trial.

On August 22, 1944, Jack and Edie had a courthouse marriage ceremony. Soon afterward, the newlyweds moved to Michigan to be near Edie's family. But Kerouac was unhappy there, and the marriage faltered almost immediately. In October 1944, Kerouac headed back to New York, leaving Edie in Michigan.

Kerouac drifted rather aimlessly in New York, sometimes staying with his parents but also temporarily moving into Ginsberg's dorm room at Columbia. Kerouac and Ginsberg read each other's writing and had long discussions about life and art. Ginsberg also kept Kerouac stocked with reading material, checking out armfuls of books for him from the university library.

During this time, Ginsberg revealed to Kerouac that he was gay—and that he was in love with Kerouac. Surprised, Kerouac said he wasn't interested in a romantic relationship with Ginsberg. But the two remained good friends.

Later in the winter of 1944, other friends moved back to New York, including Seymour Wyse, Kerouac's jazz-loving friend from Horace Mann. Kerouac and Wyse spent hours listening to jazz tunes and singing their own versions. Musical rhythms began to influence Kerouac's writing. Burroughs also rejoined the group. He shared his favorite books and authors with Kerouac and Ginsberg and joined in their literary conversations. Burroughs and Kerouac began working together on a mystery-style novel about David Kammerer's murder. They called it *And the Hippos Were Boiled in Their Tanks*.

That December Edie also returned to New York. She and Kerouac formed a tentative peace and moved in with Joan Vollmer, Edie's old roommate, who was renting a large apartment on 115th Street. In an unconventional living arrangement for the time, many men and women shared the big apartment over the following months. Burroughs moved in, and he and Vollmer struck up a romantic relationship. Ginsberg was a frequent guest and sometimes a resident, along with others who came and went. Edie herself moved in and out as she struggled to decide whether or not to continue her relationship with Kerouac. Meanwhile, she and Kerouac both dated other people. By spring 1945, the marriage was essentially over. As Kerouac put it in a letter to his sister, "I've asked Edie for a divorce, but nicely." He added, "If we do get divorced, I'll go on seeing her occasionally, for we are both wacky in a way, and we should never have gotten married but just gone on knowing each other."

At the 115th Street apartment, Kerouac became friends with Hal Chase, one of the roommates there. Chase intrigued Kerouac, in part because he came from Denver, Colorado. To Kerouac, Colorado was part of a great mythic American West that he longed to explore.

Another roommate, Vicki Russell, introduced Kerouac to the illegal drug Benzedrine. This stimulant, called bennies for short, gives the user a burst of energy and a sense of greater mental alertness. (The drug also has downsides, often causing anxiety, sleeplessness, depression, and more serious mental health problems.) Although most Americans of the 1940s considered drug use scandalous and immoral, Kerouac and most of his companions experimented with a variety of illegal drugs. Many of them smoked marijuana, and Burroughs used morphine. Kerouac found bennies especially appealing, using the high to fuel his writing. He told Ginsberg, "Benny has made me see a lot. The process of intensifying awareness naturally leads to an overflow of old notions, and voilà, new material wells up like water."

Together with the drugs came a wilder set of guests at the apartment. One of them was Herbert Huncke, a

Herbert Huncke (right) *introduced Kerouac and his friends to some of New York City's darker sides. He was such a fixture in the Times Square area—from 42nd to 47th streets along Broadway and Seventh Avenue—that he earned the nickname "Mayor of 42nd Street."*

drug addict, writer, hobo-wanderer, and part-time criminal. Kerouac later described him as "sad, sweet, dark, holy. Just out of jail. Martyred. Tortured by side-walks... open to anything, ready to introduce a new world with a shrug." Huncke spent most of his time on 42nd Street at Times Square, a seedy area of Man-hattan. Burroughs, Vollmer, and Kerouac were fasci-nated by this underbelly of the city. They sometimes prowled the area for a glimpse of life there.

During this chaotic time, Kerouac still bounced between Manhattan and his parents' place. While he tried to hide his drug use, his parents could see that he had changed. He remained very close to his mother but argued frequently with his father. Leo harshly criticized what he saw as his son's good-for-nothing friends and dead-end lifestyle.

But new sadness was near. By late 1945, Kerouac's father was battling cancer. Kerouac began living mostly at home so he could care for Leo while Gabrielle worked. "Slowly he withered before my eyes," Kerouac wrote. "My father never yelled out in pain, he just winced and groaned and wept softly, O good man of my heart."

That December Kerouac himself was hospitalized. His continued Benzedrine use had led to phlebitis—painful and dangerous blood clots in his legs. But Ker-ouac recovered while his father continued to ail. In spring 1946, Leo lost the battle—though not before insisting that his son promise to take care of Gabrielle.

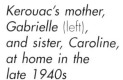

Kerouac's mother, Gabrielle (left), *and sister, Caroline, at home in the late 1940s*

And then, wrote Kerouac, "one morning after we had an argument about how to brew coffee . . . he just died in his chair right in front of my eyes."

Kerouac deeply mourned Leo's death. Although they had often been at odds, they had loved each other.

"POETRY AND NOVEL"

During the months of Leo's illness, most of the residents of Vollmer's apartment had gone their separate ways. The apartment's rotating group of friends was no longer there for Kerouac to go back to. So in 1946, at the age of twenty-four, he again made his home with Mémêre. She took a series of low-paying jobs to support herself and her son.

Kerouac still spent time near Columbia, however, and continued to meet new people. Hal Chase introduced him to Denver natives Ed White and Beverly Burford. Kerouac also became friends with an aspiring author named Allan Temko.

Around this time, Kerouac began a new writing project. While he later declared that the novel, titled *The Town and the City*, was fiction, its plot is semiautobiographical. It follows the story of the Martin family, living in the mill town of Galloway, New Hampshire. The main character, Peter, wins a football scholarship that takes him to New York City. There he makes friends with fellow students and experiences more of the world—experience that sometimes saddens him. Describing Peter's sorrow when his parents move to New York—leaving the town for the city, just as Kerouac's parents had left Lowell—Kerouac wrote, "He had known a boy's life in Galloway . . . he had known all the gravities and the glees and the wonders of life. Now all that was lost, vanished, haunted and ghostly." Kerouac also sketched fictionalized portraits of his friends. Burroughs showed up as Will Dennison, and Ginsberg became Leon Levinsky, "an eager, intense, sharply intelligent boy of Russian-Jewish parentage who rushed around New York in a perpetual sweat of emotional activity."

Kerouac's style in *The Town and the City* was influenced by writers he admired, especially Thomas Wolfe. But it was also uniquely his own. Ginsberg called the book a "great fusion of poetry and novel in America."

NEAL

While Kerouac transformed his life's cast of characters in novel form, a new and vibrant character entered the picture. Twenty-year-old Neal Cassady arrived in New York in the winter of 1946 in a burst of energy and charm, plus a dash of danger and recklessness. Cassady was an old Denver friend of Hal Chase. Kerouac saw Cassady, like Chase, as a sort of ambassador from an exciting and unknown part of the United States—a "trim, thin-hipped, blue-eyed . . . sideburned hero of the snowy West."

This charismatic newcomer fascinated Kerouac. Cassady was a free-spirited youth who had grown up poor and attended several reform schools before driving east with his beautiful sixteen-year-old wife, Luanne Henderson. In New York, he found a job—as "the most fantastic parking-lot attendant in the world," Kerouac

Neal Cassady worked as a parking attendant in New York City.

wrote. Cassady managed to make almost any activity—even parking cars—seem exciting and heroic.

After a few months in New York, Cassady came to Kerouac at Mémère's apartment, asking for writing lessons. Kerouac suspected that Cassady really just wanted a place to stay. He and Luanne had briefly rented an apartment, but Luanne had gone back to Denver after an argument. Since then, Cassady had been moving from couch to couch in various people's homes. Next, it seemed, he hoped to crash on Kerouac's couch.

But Kerouac didn't mind. He enjoyed Cassady's company and admired his confidence and vivid story-telling. Cassady was genuinely drawn to Kerouac as well, impressed by both his writing ability and his past as a college football player. Luanne would later observe that "Jack and Neal were . . . like two kids. . . . Very close and warm and discovering things together, or discovering that they liked the same things, that they had thought the same things."

Mémère was hesitant to let this unfamiliar and vaguely wild man into her home, but Kerouac convinced her to allow it. Cassady wasn't there for long, however. He soon began staying with Ginsberg and learning about writing from him too. But Cassady's visit had revived Kerouac's urge to get away from the East Coast and discover more of the United States.

Cassady returned to Colorado in March 1947.

Kerouac planned to visit him, while Cassady sent letters encouraging him to begin his trip as soon as possible. Ginsberg also headed westward, to see both
Cassady and Burroughs, who had married Joan
Vollmer and moved to Texas. The reasons were
mounting for Kerouac to act on his dreams—to take
off and seek adventure.

Kerouac hit the road in 1947, heading westward across the United
States to San Francisco, California (above).

Chapter **FOUR**

ON THE ROAD

IN THE SUMMER OF **1947,** KEROUAC FINALLY DID take off. He'd heard from Henri Cru, an old merchant marine friend, about work on a ship in San Francisco. Kerouac jumped at the chance. Short on money as usual and hungry for real adventure, he decided to hitchhike west. He chose Route 6 as his path, "one long red line" on a map, running all the way from New York to California. He left home in mid-July.

To pick up Route 6, Kerouac first had to hitchhike to Bear Mountain Bridge in upstate New York. On the bridge, traffic was light, rain was heavy, and the only ride he got landed him back in New York City. Wet, tired, and extremely frustrated, Kerouac decided to spend most of his limited funds on a bus ticket to Chicago.

The next few days were spent on an "ordinary bus trip with crying babies and hot sun." The ride took Kerouac from the East Coast's forests and dense population into the more wide-open lands of Ohio and Indiana, finally dumping him in the gray belly of Chicago. After a rest and a few hours of sightseeing, Kerouac left Chicago. Thumbing his way west, he finally caught a glimpse of the United States he'd been imagining—the open spaces of the plains and roads that "shoot west for incredible distances."

After a series of rides with truck drivers, college kids, and mothers, he crossed the great Mississippi River. But in Des Moines, Iowa, after going to sleep and waking up again in the unfamiliar city, Kerouac suddenly felt disoriented and lost. "I was far away from home, haunted and tired with travel, in a cheap hotel room I'd never seen," he wrote in *On the Road*. "I was just somebody else, some stranger, and my whole life was a haunted life, the life of a ghost. I was halfway across America, at the dividing line between the East of my youth and the West of my future."

Moving toward that future, Kerouac kept hitching rides and taking buses when no rides could be found. As he traveled, he ate a steady diet of pie and ice cream. It was cheap, and it was good. By July 24, he was in Omaha, Nebraska, where he saw a real cowboy and sent his mother a postcard. His favorite ride was the one he caught between Gothenburg, Nebraska, and Cheyenne, Wyoming, with the Minnesota farm boys.

Finally, on July 28, he reached Denver. Lying on high plains at the foot of the Rocky Mountains, the city was an impressive sight. As Colorado's capital—and home to more than three hundred thousand people—Denver was no small-town outpost. Yet as an old mining town and agricultural center—and burial place of Old West legend Buffalo Bill—it had the frontier flavor that Kerouac had been craving.

Kerouac didn't know exactly where in Denver Cassady was, but he did find Hal Chase. Soon he reconnected with the whole gang of Denverites and New Yorkers, including Ginsberg, Ed White, Allan Temko, and Beverly Burford. There were new people too, such as Cassady's friend Al Hinkle and Cassady's new girlfriend Carolyn Robinson. Though Kerouac spent only about ten days in Denver, he packed them full. He rambled around town, drinking in bars, meeting women, and playing pool in dingy halls. As always, he and Ginsberg and the others did plenty of talking, writing, and talking about writing.

Meanwhile, Kerouac recorded his experiences, scribbling countless details and observations in notebooks. His vision of exploring the United States also included the dream of writing a book about it. That book, he hoped, would capture the beauty and joy and enthusiasm and longing that he saw in his country—and that he felt within himself.

"No More Land"

Kerouac enjoyed Denver, but he had to get to San Francisco if he wanted the job Cru had promised. So after writing to ask Mémêre for bus fare, Kerouac left Denver. Reaching the West Coast in mid-August, he moved in with Cru and his girlfriend in an apartment across the bay from San Francisco. As it turned out, the expected jobs didn't exist, but Cru and Kerouac found work as security guards at a construction workers' camp. Kerouac took advantage of the camp's office typewriter to compose letters to Cassady, Ginsberg, his sister, and others. But he hated his bosses and the job, especially the duty of breaking up parties that seemed harmless enough to him. In *On the Road*, he wrote, "This is the story of America. Everybody's doing what they think they're supposed to do. So what if a bunch of men talk in loud voices and drink the night?"

Meanwhile, Cru hatched a scheme in which Kerouac would write a story, Cru would sell it to a Hollywood movie studio, and they would all be rich and famous. But nothing came of the plan. As the weeks passed, the whole situation deteriorated. Cru and his girlfriend fought often, and Kerouac and Cru also began to argue. "Everything was falling apart," Kerouac wrote. "Here I was at the end of America—no more land—and now there was nowhere to go but back." In October 1947, he did go back.

Rather than retracing his steps home, Kerouac hitchhiked and bused south to Los Angeles and then east. On the way, he met a young woman named Bea Franco. They began a sudden romance, and Kerouac spent two weeks with her. Bea was a Mexican migrant worker, and her family's extreme poverty showed Kerouac a harsher, rougher side of life than he'd ever seen. They talked of hitching to New York together. But Kerouac left her in California one morning after she made him breakfast—having used her, perhaps, as little more than an experience to write about.

Back with Mémêre in New York at the end of 1947, Kerouac returned his attention to *The Town and the City*. He also continued his correspondence with friends scattered around the country, especially Cassady—who by then had divorced Luanne and married Carolyn. Ginsberg had returned to New York, and Kerouac spent a lot of time with him. At one party in July, Kerouac met John Clellon Holmes—yet another

Kerouac met aspiring writer John Clellon Holmes (right) *in New York. The two became good friends.*

aspiring writer and soon a good friend. Burroughs visited town briefly, and Huncke was around too. Plus, there were always new people to meet and new young women to date.

Kerouac finished *The Town and the City* in May 1948 and set about trying to find a publisher. He sent the manuscript to Scribner's, which rejected it. He tried Macmillan and Little, Brown, which also turned it down. He began to grow discouraged but kept revising the manuscript and trying again. He was twenty-six years old.

TO AND FRO

In autumn 1948, Kerouac was still hoping for an acceptance letter for his first novel. While he waited, he took literature classes at the New School for Social Research in Greenwich Village. He also began a novel about his childhood, *Doctor Sax*, but grew frustrated with the work. So he turned to a different idea: a book about his travels. In late 1948, he started transforming his trip journals into a novel that would become *On the Road*.

He started composing this new book in a style similar to *The Town and the City*. But it wasn't working. John Clellon Holmes recalled, "He wrote seven, maybe ten other beginnings to the book, and they all didn't seem right to him." The style wasn't the only problem. Kerouac felt somehow that the story wasn't finished. He needed more experience and more material.

The search for a publisher of *The Town and the City*

dragged on. Ginsberg tried to help, enthusiastically recommending the book to everyone. But Kerouac, beginning to doubt his own talent, grew depressed. His letters showed his restlessness and dissatisfaction. He wrote to Cassady that winter, "I am not entirely giving up on my writing-prospect, but no longer banking on it, not a moment more."

Cassady, living with Carolyn in San Francisco, urged Kerouac to come back to California. But before that happened, Cassady got on the road himself. Leaving behind Carolyn and their new baby, Cathy, he borrowed some money and bought a car. In December 1948, he showed up in North Carolina. Kerouac and his mother were there visiting Caroline, who had remarried. Cassady was accompanied by his ex-wife, Luanne, with whom he remained romantically involved, and Al Hinkle. As 1949 opened, Kerouac also piled into the car, and all four left the East Coast for another cross-country trip.

Kerouac felt freer and happier on the road, as if he were leaving his cares behind. He enjoyed watching the country roll past his windows as the highway stretched out ahead, and he loved the hours of talking and laughing with his friends. Their first destination was New Orleans, where William and Joan Burroughs had moved. The group stayed at the Burroughs household for a few days and then headed onward through the humid Deep South, into the dry Southwest, and toward California.

Soon after they reached San Francisco, Cassady abruptly left the group to return to his wife and daughter. The remaining travelers also parted ways, leaving Kerouac to wander hungry and penniless through the city. Angry, hurt, and feeling abandoned, he decided to go home. He boarded a bus, and in February he was back on the East Coast.

The next month, the news he'd been waiting for finally arrived. Editor Robert Giroux at Harcourt Brace accepted *The Town and the City* and offered Kerouac a thousand-dollar advance (money paid before a book is completed). Kerouac was thrilled. In a letter to Ed White, he wrote, "I'm just chuckling all over." He was not so happy about some of the changes made during editing—especially the decision to cut his eleven hundred pages of text to four hundred. It turned the book, he said, "from a mighty . . . black book of sorrows into a 'saleable' ordinary novel." Nevertheless, he was mostly chuckling as his future as a published author opened before him.

In May—perhaps still hoping to capture the magic of the West—Kerouac moved to Denver. He intended for Mémêre to join him so that he could take care of her as his father had asked. But Gabrielle didn't like Colorado and soon left, while Kerouac stayed on alone, trying to make *On the Road* work. He also visited many of Cassady's old haunts. But Cassady was gone, as were most of Kerouac's other Denver acquaintances. Without anyone to share them with, the places seemed empty and sad. And even with his upcoming publication, which he had wanted so much, Kerouac felt uprooted and lost. As he put it, "There was nothing behind me anymore, all my bridges were gone and I didn't [care] about anything at all." So when Cassady asked him to come to San Francisco in July, Kerouac packed up and left.

Cassady was a mess. He was still juggling his wife and his ex-wife, as well as having other affairs. He had health problems, which were worsened by heavy drinking. But Kerouac's visit made him happy, and in August they hit the road again, with vague plans to visit Europe. They sped across the country toward New York, talking nearly nonstop, with a crazy energy and enthusiasm sometimes fueled by drugs. Cassady's unpredictable behavior—chasing women, stealing cars for joyrides on a whim, and driving at outrageous speeds—made the journey a dangerous but exhilarating whirlwind. When they reached New York in October—somehow getting there safely and without being arrested—Kerouac was exhausted. Cassady soon moved in with a new girlfriend.

Kerouac, as always, returned to his writing and to Mémère. When he showed up at her door, time and time again and often penniless, she was sometimes stern with him. She disapproved of his friends, and mother and son often argued. But Mémère was also deeply protective of her Ti Jean, and the two remained very close. Ultimately, Mémère always welcomed her son back into her home.

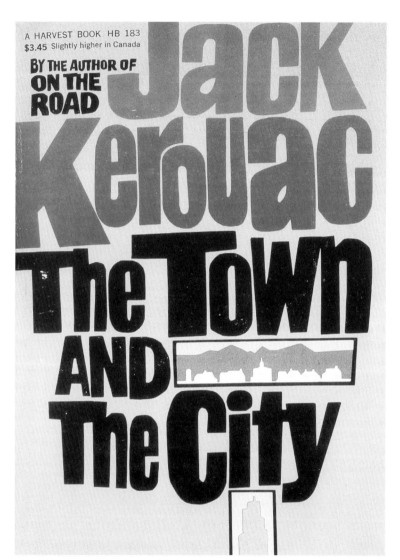

A HARVEST BOOK HB 183
$3.45 Slightly higher in Canada

BY THE AUTHOR OF
ON THE ROAD

JaCK
Kerouac

The Town
AND
The City

Kerouac's first book, The Town and the City, was published in 1950.

Chapter **FIVE**

PUBLISHED

THE *TOWN AND THE CITY* WAS RELEASED IN EARLY
1950. The book was not the instant success that Kerouac had fantasized about. Reviews were mixed and sales were low. Nevertheless, at first he enjoyed his role as a published writer, with a handsome author photo and book signings to attend.

Soon the old doubts and restlessness returned, however, and in June Kerouac hopped on a bus to Denver. He spent a calm visit there with Ed White and Beverly Burford, until Cassady arrived with plans to travel to Mexico and get a divorce from Carolyn. The two men arranged to go to Mexico City, where they would visit William and Joan Burroughs, who had moved again. Cassady drove them south in his usual fast and wild way. They crossed the border ready for adventure.

Almost as soon as they reached Mexico, Kerouac fell ill with dysentery, an intestinal disease. He recovered at the Burroughses' home, while Cassady headed back to the United States to marry his new girlfriend. Kerouac stayed on in Mexico. He frequently smoked marijuana, which was readily available, cheap, and strong. Burroughs sometimes joined him, engaging him in long discussions. Other times, Kerouac wandered the streets of Mexico City alone. He tried to write. But while he believed the drugs increased his creativity, they also interfered with his concentration, and he made little progress. At the end of the summer, he decided it was time to leave. Hitchhiking most of the way to Long Island, he moved back in with Mémère.

JACK AND JOAN

Early in the winter of 1950, Kerouac met a friend of Ginsberg's named Joan Haverty. Only two weeks later, in mid-November, they were married. Jack was twenty-eight years old, and Joan was twenty. In *On the Road*, Kerouac wrote about their fast-paced romance. The night they met, he wrote, he saw her as "the girl with the pure and innocent dear eyes that I had always searched for. . . . We agreed to love each other madly."

But only about six months after they were married, Kerouac and Haverty separated. The split had several causes. Kerouac expected his wife to tend to his

Kerouac's second wife, Joan Haverty, was also a writer. Although she did not publish any books during her lifetime, she did complete a memoir titled Nobody's Wife.

needs, handling the cooking, cleaning, and other household chores. Haverty probably found it difficult to cope with Kerouac's unemployment. And when Haverty found that she was pregnant, Kerouac said he didn't want the baby and claimed that he wasn't the father. Haverty was on her own.

The marriage was abruptly over. Kerouac later summed up the entire relationship in a few cold words: "I didn't like her. She didn't like any of my friends. My friends didn't like her. But she was beautiful. I married her because she was beautiful."

A RUSH OF WORDS

Throughout the beginning and breakup of his second marriage, Kerouac had gone back to *On the Road*.

Having crisscrossed the country several times, he finally felt he had enough material. But he was still frustrated. The narrative prose of traditional novels seemed too rigid and constricting for the story he was trying to tell. He wanted something new and different. In the winter of 1950–1951, he found it in a lengthy letter from Cassady. The letter, which described a long-past adventure, was fluid, frank, and energetic. It seemed as though Cassady had poured his thoughts right onto the paper.

The Joan Anderson Letter, as it was later called, stunned Kerouac. He wrote back to Cassady that he considered it "among the best things ever written in America." To Kerouac, the letter showed the future of American literature, revealing the new form he'd been searching for. This discovery marked the beginning of a style that he would eventually call spontaneous prose. Newly inspired, he tried yet another approach to writing *On the Road*.

In April 1951, he threaded his typewriter with a long spool of paper, sat down at his desk, and began to write. And write. He wrote almost constantly for the next three weeks. Barely sleeping, energized by coffee and Benzedrine, Kerouac typed thousands upon thousands of words. By the end of the month, he was finished.

Thrilled with his new style and the resulting book, Kerouac showed the manuscript to both John Clellon Holmes and Allen Ginsberg. Both were impressed, and

A thirty-six-foot section of Kerouac's On the Road *scroll—the original manuscript for the book—was on display at the San Francisco Main Library in January 2006.*

Holmes admired Kerouac's "enormous capacity for sense impressions and his gift for catching them on the fly." Holmes was also amazed at Kerouac's writing method. "He wanted to break loose and he didn't want to have to pause for anything, so he wrote *On the Road* in one long paragraph," recalled Holmes. "He just flung it down." Describing the book to Cassady in May, Kerouac wrote, "Story deals with you and me and the road. . . . Went fast because road is fast."

In reworking that story, Kerouac had made Cassady the book's hero and himself its narrator. (He originally used real names, but in later versions, Cassady became Dean Moriarty and Kerouac was Sal Paradise.) In three main parts, the book described the friends' trips between 1947 and 1950. It detailed Kerouac's hitchhiking adventures, the wild times he spent with Cassady, the ups and downs of life on the road, and the many people he encountered in his travels.

Kerouac rushed the manuscript to Robert Giroux, the editor of *The Town and the City*. But Giroux was not interested in a many-feet-long paragraph full of real people's names and little punctuation. He rejected it in June.

Hurt and angry, Kerouac wrote to Cassady, "My soul is hungup right now & I gotta make a move soon." But he had neither the money nor the opportunity to move. That summer he developed phlebitis again. Meanwhile, Haverty asked him for money to support the child she was carrying. He refused.

Kerouac kept on writing. In October he explored a new method that he called sketching. It grew out of a conversation with his friend Ed White, who proposed trying to write in the way an artist quickly draws a scene. Kerouac had seized the idea, which let his creativity take over and freed him to write without constraints.

Still, the old itch to travel remained. In December 1951, Kerouac bused to San Francisco and moved in

Kerouac in 1952 with Neal Cassady's wife, Carolyn, and two of her children, Cathy (left) *and Jamie* (right).

with Cassady (who was then living with Carolyn and their three children). Kerouac enjoyed spending time with Carolyn and the kids, going out on the town with Neal, and writing in his attic room. As 1952 began, he worked on a project he called *Visions of Neal.* (Its final name would be *Visions of Cody.*)

Some sections of *Visions of Cody* followed *On the Road*'s basic story line, with Cassady still the star. But *Visions* was far more committed to Kerouac's ever-evolving idea of spontaneous prose. Sentences sometimes stretched for half a page or more, and whole sections of dialogue were transcribed from tape recordings. It also used his sketching technique extensively. The opening scene depicts an old diner in vivid detail. Kerouac describes "stools with smooth slickwood tops" and the odor of "boiling beef, like the smell of the great kitchens of parochial boarding schools or old hospitals."

RUNNING AND WRITING

As Kerouac worked on *Visions of Cody* in San Francisco, Ginsberg was in New York trying to sell *On the Road*. He made an informal agreement with a publishing house where his friend Carl Solomon worked. He even secured Kerouac a $250 advance. But the arrangement faltered when Kerouac insisted that his manuscript needed no revision. In the end, his stubbornness doomed the deal.

Kerouac also faced personal problems. On February 16, 1952, Joan Haverty gave birth to Janet Michelle Kerouac in Albany, New York. But Kerouac did not visit his daughter. Nor would he send money for her care.

Some sources suggest that Kerouac refused to support his daughter because he wanted to take care of his mother—who still helped support him—and was worried about running out of money. Others propose that he was unwilling to grow up and accept responsibility. Still others suggest that he was simply insensitive and uncaring.

Whatever his reasons, Kerouac's refusal to pay limited his freedom. Investigators, trying to collect money on Haverty's behalf, were on the lookout for him in New York, so he decided to avoid the city for a while. That was easy enough to do when he was content and productive in the West. His writing was going well, and he finished a draft of *Visions of Cody* around March. Later that spring, while visiting Burroughs in Mexico City, Kerouac sent a neatly typed copy of *Visions of Cody* to Ginsberg, hoping he would have better luck selling this novel. Kerouac felt that it might be even better than *On the Road*.

Kerouac next returned to *Doctor Sax*, the novel about his childhood that he had outlined years earlier. Applying his spontaneous prose method to the book, he finished it around June 1952. Meanwhile, he rediscovered the lure of Mexican marijuana.

Later that summer, Burroughs departed for South America. Kerouac headed back to North Carolina, where Mémêre was living with Caroline. But he was unhappy and restless. As autumn approached, Cassady convinced him to come work as a railroad brakeman in California. Kerouac, who had a romantic vision of railroad work, accepted. He didn't turn out to be especially good at the job. And tensions ran high between him and the Cassadys. After a few weeks, he packed his things yet again, made a brief detour to Mexico, and returned to the East Coast in late 1952.

Kerouac reading at Neal and Carolyn Cassady's home in 1954.

Chapter **SIX**

BEAT

IN AUTUMN 1952, JOHN CLELLON HOLMES HAD
published a book and an article that used the phrase
"Beat Generation." This phrase was one that Kerouac
had first used, while talking to Holmes around 1948.
At the time, he had used the phrase casually. But after
Holmes's writings were released, the name stuck.

Holmes's article defined the term *beat*, as in the
phrase "I'm beat," as meaning "more than mere weari-
ness." Being beat, he said, "implies the feeling of having been used, of being raw." Holmes went on to apply
the word to a portion of American youths who rejected
their parents' conventional values. In some cases, that
rejection included drug use and criminal activity. But
more generally, it simply meant a yearning to break

free of the era's rigid mind-sets and fears. For Kerouac, the term *beat* had a different meaning. He had picked up the word from Herbert Huncke a few years earlier. Huncke had used the adjective to describe a person who lived mostly on the street and was broke, usually addicted to drugs, and had little hope of improving his

AGAINST THE GRAIN

hen Kerouac was writing in the 1940s and 1950s, American society was generally very conservative. People valued conformity and responsibility more than individuality and carefree living. Many Americans saw freethinking artists and writers—such as Kerouac and his friends—as threatening and suspicious.

Suspicion was also a strong political force at the time. Following World War II, the U.S. government became strongly anti-Communist. (Communism, an economic and political system used in the Soviet Union, China, and other nations, is based on the idea of government-owned and -controlled businesses rather than private property.) By the early 1950s, the fear of Communism had reached a fever pitch in the United States. Even friends and neighbors suspected one another of Communist sympathies.

In this fearful climate, anyone who disregarded traditional norms and mainstream thought seemed dangerous. Members of the Beat Generation fit into that category. Their drug taking, spur-of-the-moment travels, sexual affairs, and creative works stood in stark contrast to the prevailing straitlaced culture. Some observers stereotyped all Beats as immoral and harmful to society.

or her situation. Over time, Kerouac would take the term in different directions. He linked it to the word *upbeat* and to a musical beat, referring to the jazz that so deeply influenced his writing.

All these ideas blended into a complex term that referred to a variety of things—a literary style, a lifestyle, a whole group of people. Over time, the name *Beat Generation* was applied to Kerouac's circle of writers, artists, and other characters. Kerouac, Ginsberg, and Burroughs formed the literary core of the Beats. And while Kerouac was frequently called King of the Beats, he was a reluctant leader. One friend later said, he "never wanted to be part of a social and cultural movement. He wanted to be a writer."

PLUGGING AWAY

The Beat Generation's unwilling "king" was hardly living the life of royalty. *On the Road* still sat unwanted, and *Visions of Cody* had also been rejected.

Nevertheless, in early 1953, Kerouac began work on yet another book. This one, titled first *Springtime Mary* and eventually *Maggie Cassidy*, told the tale of a romance between two small-town teenagers. Like Kerouac's other work, it was drawn from his own life. The girl in the story was modeled after his own first love, Mary Carney. He quickly finished the book, quickly submitted it to a publisher—and quickly received a rejection slip.

At this point, Kerouac decided to hire Phyllis

Jackson, a professional agent, to market his books. She arranged a lunch between Kerouac and Malcolm Cowley, an employee at Viking Press. Cowley became a great champion of *On the Road* and worked hard to convince Viking to publish it.

Meanwhile, Kerouac's personal life remained messy. By this time, he had started to drink too much alcohol. He was unsure of himself and his talent, envious of more successful authors, and depressed about his future. He used Benzedrine frequently, especially when he began another book in the fall. This work explored his intense but short-lived romance with a young African American woman in New York. In just three October nights, he cranked out a story about their brief and doomed relationship, a book he called *The Subterraneans*. The woman and man in the book are named Mardou Fox and Leo Percepied.

Kerouac was proud of his new book's spontaneity and depth of emotion. Ginsberg and Burroughs also liked the manuscript. The real woman on whom Mardou Fox was based, however, was far less pleased. In her view, the book's details were intimate and embarrassing—not to mention largely inaccurate. She felt Kerouac had exploited her to further his writing.

DREAMS AND NIGHTMARES

At the end of 1953, Kerouac felt isolated. Ginsberg was planning a trip to California and perhaps South America, while Burroughs was bound for North

Beat 69

BE MORE SPONTANEOUS!

 ny reader of Jack Kerouac's writing will soon notice long sentences, unusual capitalization, and unique punctuation. These qualities are some of the trademarks of his spontaneous prose writing technique, which came to Kerouac "after reading the marvelous free-narrative letters of Neal Cassady." Kerouac admired Cassady's overall disregard for literary formalities. Instead, as Cassady said, he set down one "continuous chain of undisciplined thought." Kerouac's technique also drew inspiration from the rhythms and patterns of jazz, especially bebop, a highly improvisational jazz form.

As spontaneous prose evolved, Kerouac compiled the "Essentials of Spontaneous Prose." The list put forth suggestions such as using "no periods separating sentence—structures already. . . riddled by false colons and timid usually needless commas." He also composed "Belief and Technique for Modern Prose," a list of tips for modern American writing. They include the following:

1. Scribbled secret notebooks, and wild typewritten pages, for your own joy

4. Be in love with yr life

19. Accept loss forever

21. Struggle to sketch the flow that already exists intact in mind

Africa. Holmes was gone too, having moved to Connecticut. Lonely and miserable, Kerouac suffered crippling self-doubt during his waking hours and terrible dreams when he slept. He drank heavily and sank into a deep depression.

As 1954 opened, Kerouac once again got on the move, traveling back to California and staying with the Cassadys in San Jose. While there, he sought answers to his restlessness, uncertainty, and feelings of fear and sadness. In early 1954, he began seeking peace in a new place—the Asian religion of Buddhism.

Kerouac had become interested in Buddhism almost by chance after stumbling across a book about it at the San Jose Library. Feeling that he had reached a low point in his life, he responded to the Buddhist idea that all existence is suffering. He took up meditation, a mental practice meant to bring about a feeling of peace and spiritual awareness.

Meanwhile, his relationship with Cassady was strained. He left the Cassadys in March after one especially bitter argument. Moving into a crummy San Francisco hotel, he began composing a set of mournful poems called *San Francisco Blues*. He also worked on a *Book of Dreams*, which was just that—a record of his dreams.

In April Kerouac returned to New York, feeling a little calmer. But his closest friends were still gone. His drug and alcohol abuse worsened, and the phlebitis in his legs flared up, forcing him to quit a new job at the Brooklyn docks. Resting at his mother's home, he undertook new writing projects, including a science-fiction story. He gained some attention when an article by Viking editor Malcolm Cowley hailed him as the inventor of the label *Beat Generation*. He received even more attention when Cowley sold excerpts from

On the Road and *Visions of Cody* to *New World Writing*, a respected journal. *On the Road* itself still lacked a publisher, but Kerouac had found a new agent, Sterling Lord, and hoped he might sell the book.

Still, the ups and downs were relentless. In October 1954, Kerouac visited Lowell. Entering a Catholic church there, he had a moment of understanding. He decided that *beat* meant not only "tired and run down" but also "beatific—holy and illuminated." Yet, returning to New York, he wrote in December that he had reached "the lowest beat ebb."

Kerouac was broke and frustrated by his continuing failure to be published. He felt trapped. And in January 1955, he was called to court to face Joan Haverty's claims for child support. His daughter was nearly three years old, and he had never even gone to see her.

In February Kerouac joined Mémêre, Caroline, and Caroline's family in North Carolina. There he wrote about Buddhism, played with his nephew, and peacefully tended a vegetable garden as he waited for word from Sterling Lord. But when the news came, it was bad—*On the Road* had been rejected again.

That April, however, the excerpts that Cowley had sold appeared in *New World Writing* under the title, "Jazz of the Beat Generation." By summer Kerouac was on an upswing. Cowley assured him that he was still interested in *On the Road*. Cowley also helped Kerouac earn a small grant—a sum of money to fund his writing—from the Academy of Arts and Letters. And a magazine accepted another short piece for publication.

In August Kerouac hitchhiked to Mexico City, where he hung out with Burroughs's friend Bill Garver. He also immersed himself in drugs and poetry. Smoking marijuana and sometimes injecting morphine, he composed a series of 242 jazzlike poems, which he called choruses. He named the collection *Mexico City Blues*. In addition to drawing on musical influences, the poems incorporated Buddhist ideas and Kerouac's sketching technique. Kerouac also began writing *Tristessa*, a short novel describing Kerouac's relationship with a Mexican prostitute.

Seeking Dharma

Leaving Mexico in the fall, Kerouac headed north to Berkeley, California, where Ginsberg was then living. Kerouac met Ginsberg's new friends, a group of poets responsible for a surge of creative activity known as the San Francisco Renaissance. The core group in this renaissance included Gary Snyder, Lawrence Ferlinghetti, Kenneth Rexroth, Philip Whalen, Kenneth Patchen, Jack Spicer, and Michael McClure. Like the original Beat circle in New York, these writers shared their work and their thoughts on writing with one another. Ferlinghetti founded his own bookstore and small publishing house, City Lights. When Kerouac arrived, Ginsberg first publicly performed his famous long poem "Howl," a controversial masterpiece.

Kerouac was still drinking a great deal of alcohol.

(Left to right) *Bob Donlin, Neal Cassady, Allen Ginsberg, Robert LaVigne, and Lawrence Ferlinghetti stand outside City Lights bookstore in 1956. The store still does business on Columbus Avenue in San Francisco's North Beach neighborhood.*

But he was happy to see Ginsberg, and he enjoyed the company of this vibrant new group of poets. He became especially close to Snyder. Both men were interested in Buddhism, and in October they took a camping trip in Yosemite National Park. Together they hiked, discussed religion, and meditated in the clear mountain air. To Kerouac, Snyder was like a *bhikkhu*—a wandering Buddhist monk. Kerouac also called him a dharma bum, a reference to the Buddhist concept of dharma, or religious teachings.

When 1956 began, Kerouac was back in North Carolina revisiting old, sad memories. He had been over-
come with thoughts of his brother, Gerard, and
started writing *Visions of Gerard*. Sitting at Caroline's
kitchen table, high on bennies, he spent about two
weeks handwriting memories of his lost brother. The
result was a short, melancholy tale.

The situation at Caroline's was tense. Her husband
thought Kerouac was little more than a lazy drunk.
Wanting to escape—and perhaps hoping to reclaim the
peace he'd felt in the mountains with Snyder—Kerouac
applied for a job with the Washington State Forest
Service. He was offered a position as a fire lookout,
scouting for forest fires from atop a mountain. In
March he began hitchhiking back to the West Coast.

DESOLATION

In June Kerouac began his job with the forest service.
He was stationed on Desolation Peak, in Washington's
Mount Baker National Forest. And *desolation* was the
right word. Kerouac spent the next nine weeks utterly
alone. While the natural scenery surrounding his lookout tower was gorgeous, boredom and loneliness
played tricks with his mind, and he was glad to come
down from the mountain in September.

Back in San Francisco, he rejoined the city's
community of poets, including Ginsberg, Ginsberg's
boyfriend Peter Orlovsky, and their friend Gregory
Corso. By then the San Francisco writers were

rebelling against what they saw as a stuffy literary "establishment." Kerouac had little interest in their mission. He simply wanted to write. He soon left for Mexico City, where he finished *Tristessa* and began *Desolation Angels*, a book about his time on Desolation Peak. He also received good news from his agent: the *Evergreen Review* magazine, owned by Grove Press, wanted to publish *The Subterraneans*.

FAME GLIMMERS ON THE HORIZON

By November Kerouac was back on the East Coast. There he received the best news yet: Viking Press had agreed to publish *On the Road*.

In the almost ten years since he had begun *On the Road*, Kerouac had written six more novels, a couple of volumes of poetry, and many other pieces. He and his circle of friends had reached a crossroads—they were about to become famous. Early in 1957, the *Evergreen Review* published an issue focusing on the San Francisco writers. The *New York Times* had also printed articles on San Francisco's literary scene. Ferlinghetti's City Lights had published Ginsberg's *Howl and Other Poems*, which had gained significant attention, from praise to outrage. The Beat writers had been around for a while, but a much wider audience was suddenly taking notice.

Kerouac met up with many friends on a trip to Morocco in 1957. They included, Peter Orlovsky and Paul Bowles (left to right, sitting)*; and William Burroughs, Allen Ginsberg, Alan Ansen, Gregory Corso, and Ian Sommerville* (left to right, standing)*. The trip was Kerouac's longest journey at that time.*

Chapter **SEVEN**

FAME AND MISFORTUNE

IN NEW YORK IN EARLY **1957,** KEROUAC BEGAN dating an aspiring writer named Joyce Glassman. But Kerouac soon departed on his longest journey yet. In February he traveled by ship to Tangier, Morocco, to see Burroughs. As the ocean voyage neared its end and Tangier came into view, Kerouac marveled at the unfamiliar North African landscape. He described the scene in *Desolation Angels*. "When we first saw the pale motleys of yellow sand and green meadow which marked the vague little coast line of Africa ... I saw the white roofs of the little port of Tangiers sitting right there in the elbow of the land, on the water. This dream of white robed Africa on the blue afternoon Sea, wow, who dreamed it?"

Kerouac's first days in Morocco were pleasant. The sun was warm, Kerouac enjoyed seeing Burroughs, and Ginsberg and Peter Orlovsky soon joined them. Yet as time passed, Kerouac felt a growing sense of despair and disillusionment. His use of opium and other drugs didn't help, only making him nervous and ill-tempered. He wrote in *Desolation Angels,* "It was on this trip that the great change took place in my life which I called a complete turningabout . . . from a youthful brave sense of adventure to a complete nausea concerning experience in the world." He went on, "avoid the World, it's just a lot of dust and drag and means nothing in the end."

Another frustration in Tangier was what Kerouac saw as an attack on his talent. Grove Press's *Evergreen Review* was still planning to print *The Subterraneans,* but editor Don Allen had changed the text significantly. When Kerouac received the revision in March, he was angry and offended. To his agent, Sterling Lord, he wrote furiously, "I'd rather die than betray my faith in my work, which is inseparable from my life." "The manuscript," he complained, "is no longer THE SUB-TERRANEANS by Jack K but some feeble something by Don Allen—He apparently thinks that I dont know what I'm doing." In the end, Grove Press agreed to print a different piece by Kerouac in the magazine and to publish *The Subterraneans* as a book instead.

In April Kerouac left Africa, heading north across the Mediterranean Sea to France. But a European vacation did not suit his mood either, and he soon went back to the United States. He joined Mémère in Orlando, Florida, where Caroline's family had moved. Finding himself unable to write in Florida, however, he soon took a trip to Mexico City. It was a miserable stay. His old friend Garver had died, his girlfriend "Tristessa" was nowhere to be found, and Kerouac fell ill with a terrible fever. The last straw was an earthquake. Terrified and haunted by visions of his own death, Kerouac hurried back to Orlando.

ON THE EDGE

In September 1957, *On the Road* was finally published. It was due to hit bookstores on September 5. But Kerouac was stuck in Florida—a thousand miles from the action in New York and too broke to afford bus fare. So he called Joyce Glassman and asked her for a loan. As soon as she sent him the thirty dollars he needed, he hopped on a Greyhound bus.

By September 4, Kerouac was in New York City with Joyce. Late that night, the couple walked to a little newsstand. They knew that a review of *On the Road* would appear in the next morning's *New York Times*, which was available after midnight. Standing on the darkened street, they opened the paper to the Books of the Times section.

On the Road's "publication is a historic occasion," wrote reviewer Gilbert Millstein. The novel "is the most beautifully executed, the clearest and the most important utterance yet made by the generation. . . Looking to the future." Millstein went on, "It seems certain that 'On the Road' will come to be known as [the testament] of the 'Beat Generation.'. . . 'On the Road' is a major novel."

That night Kerouac was once again filled with great dreams and ideas and hopes. A bit stunned by the glowing review, he went home to sleep. As Glassman later wrote, nothing would be the same for Kerouac again. "Jack lay down obscure for the last time in his life. The ringing phone woke him the next morning and he was famous."

THE WEIGHT OF FAME

The sudden stardom that *On the Road* brought Kerouac was something he had longed for. At last, it seemed that his talent and the originality of his style were being recognized. His work was praised by one of the most respected newspapers in the country. Yet the very night that he and Glassman read the *New York Times* review, Kerouac sensed how unprepared he actually was for the attention. "Jack kept shaking his head," Glassman remembered. "He didn't look happy, exactly, but strangely puzzled, as if he couldn't figure out why he wasn't happier than he was."

Kerouac did find fame exciting at first. He went to parties, spoke with admirers, and dated women who were attracted by his celebrity. But it soon became clear that fame conflicted with Kerouac's basic nature as a shy, reflective person. Suddenly he faced interviews by newspapers, magazines, television, and radio.

One of the many photo shoots Kerouac endured for publicity after On the Road *was published in 1957*

He received passionate fan mail, along with biting criticism. Soon his agent was promising movie deals, public readings, and more. It was all too much.

Shortly after Millstein's *New York Times* review appeared, Millstein threw a party in Kerouac's honor. But Kerouac, sick and overwhelmed, could not bring himself to go. Instead, he called John Clellon Holmes and begged him to come over. Holmes arrived to find Kerouac in a state of utter confusion. "He'd been interviewed by television people five or six times, newspaper people. He didn't know who he was, and he was just terrified. He was lying there in bed, holding his head."

Young people, in particular, fell in love with *On the Road*, drawn to its ideas of freedom and throwing off social expectations. But they were also drawn to Kerouac—this intelligent, handsome man whose true adventures sounded so much more exciting than most readers' lives. Kerouac himself became more of a star than his book. Strangers began showing up at his house, desperate to see him, touch him, even steal one of his notebooks.

FROM BEAT TO BEATNIK

n 1958 the media coined the name *beatnik*. First used by Herb Caen, a writer for the *San Francisco Chronicle*, it was initially an insulting term for the original Beats. Over time, however, *beatnik* came to refer to "young people who modeled themselves on the *Beats*." Following the publication of Ginsberg's *Howl* and the success of *On the Road*, some fans adopted the trappings of the Beat lifestyle.

Young people gather at a beatnik hangout, The Gas House, in Los Angeles, California, in 1959.

In New York City, especially Greenwich Village, students, artists, musicians, and writers gathered in coffeehouses to socialize and listen to poetry. Stereotypical beatniks, as featured in movies, television shows, and the public imagination, dressed in black, sported goatees (if they were men) or leotards (if they were women), and smoked marijuana. While this image was a caricature, it was founded in some truth. And while Kerouac and most of his friends despised the term, many beatniks embraced it.

Holmes later explained, "Most books that come out are contained. That is, 'I want to read that book.' But what happened when *On the Road* came out was, 'I want to know that man.' It wasn't the book so much as it was the man. [Kerouac] became more and more confused as it went on."

Also upsetting for Kerouac was that not all the attention was good. The book was selling fantastically, but most reviews were less positive than Millstein's. One famous criticism came from the prominent and popular author Truman Capote, who said during a television interview that Kerouac's work was "not writing, it's just . . . typing!"

As Kerouac became the Beat Generation's unwilling spokesperson, some critics accused him and his friends of being immoral. Others made fun of him and his ideas. And Kerouac's own words were sometimes twisted in ways he didn't expect. In interviews, Kerouac spoke earnestly and energetically about his writing, beliefs, and passions. But it seemed to him that most interviewers and audiences didn't understand what he was saying. Unable to handle the harsh glare of the spotlight, Kerouac began drinking more heavily than ever. To summon the courage to do further interviews, he frequently drank beforehand—which only made matters worse.

In addition, Kerouac did not always present things with complete accuracy. For example, in describing how he had written *On the Road*, he focused on the three weeks when he had typed the scroll in a rush of frantic productivity. This account was true, but Kerouac neglected to mention that he'd worked on the book for years beforehand. Nevertheless, the story became part of *On the Road*'s legend, feeding the public's fascination with its author.

PRESSURES AND PAINS

As *On the Road* continued to sell in huge numbers, Kerouac's publisher and editor pressured him for another book. But they didn't want works as unconventional as *Doctor Sax* or *Visions of Cody*. They were hungry for another best seller. So in autumn and early winter 1957, staying in Orlando, Kerouac wrote what he thought they wanted. The result was *The Dharma Bums*. The book describes Kerouac's time with Gary Snyder in California, their hiking trip in the mountains, and their exploration of Buddhism. Viking accepted the book for publication. Meanwhile, Kerouac worked on a play called *The Beat Generation* and a novel called *Memory Babe*.

Kerouac's next book to come out was *The Subterraneans*, released by Grove Press in February 1958. The reception was poor, and Kerouac was especially stung by harsh criticism from Kenneth Rexroth, one of the San Francisco Renaissance poets. Nevertheless, the book sold many copies. A movie studio even bought rights to the story.

Kerouac also took on new projects, including a recording of him reading his work, backed by piano.

Meanwhile, he kept drinking, sometimes sitting at home in front of the television. Other times he went to bars, where he began getting into arguments and occasionally fistfights. Kerouac rarely fought back when attacked. Once he was beaten so badly that he needed stitches.

Fame certainly had not brought Kerouac happiness. It was, however, bringing in some money. Using that income, Kerouac thought he might finally stop wandering. In spring 1958, he bought a house in Northport, New York, for him and his mother. The town was close enough to New York City that Kerouac could visit friends there, but it was a quiet community that might offer some calm. He moved into the home with Mémêre and one or two cats. Mémêre handled their financial matters, screened his calls, and sorted his mail.

The next October, *The Dharma Bums* was published. About the same time, Kerouac and Glassman broke up. Kerouac was growing more and more isolated at his home with Mémêre.

In early 1959, however, he collaborated with Ginsberg, Orlovsky, Corso, and others on a film called *Pull My Daisy*. The movie depicted a failed dinner party and included a largely improvised narration by Kerouac. *Doctor Sax* was published in April 1959, and *Maggie Cassidy* came out in July. That fall *Mexico City Blues*—Kerouac's first published book of poetry—came out. But none of the works received much praise.

FACE TO FACE WITH HIMSELF

Home in Northport in early 1960, Kerouac's drinking
continued to spiral out of control. He sometimes consumed as much as a quart of alcohol every day. He alien-
ated friends, gave critics more reasons to attack him, and
made a fool of himself in public. Yet when he tried to
stop drinking, he suffered terrible withdrawal symptoms
including hallucinations, trembling, and confusion.

Even as he deteriorated, his unpublished material con-
tinued to be released. That spring a limited edition of
Visions of Cody came out, followed in June by *Tristessa*.
About this time, a studio released the movie version of
The Subterraneans. But Kerouac was dismayed that the
moviemakers had changed many aspects of the story.

Meanwhile, Kerouac struggled to write something new.
He felt he needed solitude. That summer Lawrence Ferlinghetti offered to let him stay and work at his small
cabin in Big Sur. This wilderness region along central
California's coast is renowned for its natural beauty.

Kerouac grasped desperately at the chance to steady
himself. But Big Sur would prove to do the opposite.
Once Kerouac was settled in the little cabin, the isola-
tion and the land's ruggedness were overwhelming.
After three weeks alone, fearing he was losing his
mind, he escaped to San Francisco. After drinking
with acquaintances in the city, he decided to visit Cassady. It had been several years since the friends had
seen each other, and their reunion was awkward at
first. The old easiness between them seemed to have

faded. But soon they were partying and drinking, bringing a whole group back to the little cabin at Big Sur. The next few weeks were a blur of drunken celebration alternating with agonizing withdrawal. As the days dragged on, Kerouac grew increasingly paranoid, thinking friends were trying to poison him or drive him mad. As summer ended, he dissolved into a mess of nerves and unclear thought, his mental health seriously shaken. In September he left the terror of Big Sur behind and returned to Mémère in Northport.

Late that month, a collection of writings titled *Lonesome Traveler* was published. Near the end of the year, City Lights released *Book of Dreams*. Early in 1961, Joan Haverty sued him again for child support. Kerouac did have some money by this point but still felt he owed it to his mother. He continued to deny that Janet Kerouac was his daughter—even though she looked remarkably like him.

Kerouac spent the summer of 1961 in Mexico City, working on what would become the second part of *Desolation Angels*. Covering the months after he had came down from the mountain, this section of the book described his travels to Mexico and Morocco. In September, joining Mémère and Caroline in Orlando, he began a completely new work. In ten days, using Benzedrine, he wrote the novel *Big Sur*. Confronting Kerouac's nightmare the previous summer and his deterioration in the face of fame, the book was a dark and sorrowful one. As 1961 ended, it seemed to match Kerouac's mood.

Kerouac had some professional success but many personal tragedies in the 1960s.

Chapter **EIGHT**

END OF THE ROAD

JACK KEROUAC BEGAN **1962** WITH A MONTHLONG drinking binge in New York City. It was both a celebration of completing *Big Sur* and another stage of Kerouac's alcoholism. Over the next few months, Haverty's child support lawsuit against him was wrapped up. It was on this trip that he met his daughter for the first time. Janet Michelle Kerouac—who went by Jan—was then ten years old. In March Kerouac finally agreed to help support the girl.

The rest of that year was a shifting blur. Kerouac bounced between New York and Florida. In September he spent several days in Lowell, where he hung out in local bars, tried to impress young fans, and saw old acquaintances—most of whom were horrified by his drinking and his deteriorating physical condition. Once so full of life and eagerness, Kerouac had become a tired, overweight man who suffered blackouts and seemed far older than his forty years.

Nevertheless, 1962 was punctuated by a couple of positive events. In the spring, a publisher accepted *Visions of Gerard*, and in September *Big Sur* was released. That winter he began writing *Vanity of Duluoz*. Another chapter in Kerouac's grand vision of the Duluoz Legend, the novel explored the years between his graduation from high school and his father's death.

Loss

As 1962 ended, Kerouac's writing slowed again. He was still drinking but had fewer wild binges. He visited with friends, including his old girlfriend Joyce Glassman and Cassady, who came east in the summer of 1963. *Visions of Gerard* came out in the fall but met with dismal reviews.

The next summer, in August 1964, Kerouac and his mother moved to Saint Petersburg, Florida. They were glad to be away from the stream of visitors who had come to their Northport home seeking a glimpse of Kerouac—some even peering in the windows. Mémère was also happy to be close to Caroline again. Kerouac thought the distance from the New York scene might help him work on *Vanity of Duluoz*, which was going slowly. But tragedy struck soon after they arrived. On

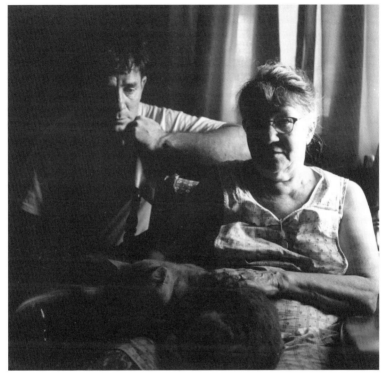

© Ann Charters

Kerouac and his mother (right) *remained close even as Kerouac's alcoholism consumed him.*

September 19, Caroline died suddenly of a heart attack. She was only forty-five years old.

That fall and winter, Kerouac tried to fend off his sorrow over his sister's death, visiting bars and playing pool. But it didn't work. Instead, one acquaintance remembered, Kerouac "was so sad he could hardly look anyone in the eye without bursting into tears."

BEAT VOICES

While the Beat authors had much in common, each had a unique style. Allen Ginsberg's poetry, for instance, is vivid, imaginative, and dreamlike. Some of his poems deal with deeply personal and disturbing subjects. "Kaddish," for example, laments his mother's death following a long struggle with mental illness. Ginsberg's most famous work is "Howl." This long poem's discussion of drugs, sex, and dark aspects of American society shocked many readers when it was published. In fact, the authorities arrested publisher Lawrence Ferlinghetti and charged him with obscenity for releasing the work. (Ferlinghetti won the case.)

William Burroughs also developed a distinctive literary voice. His semiautobiographical novels *Junkie* and *Queer* are marked by dark humor and frank discussions of drug abuse. Like Kerouac, Burroughs also explored unconventional approaches to writing, such as the "cut-up" method. This technique involved literally cutting up existing texts, such as magazines and books, and splicing together the cut-apart lines to create new, often nonsensical text. Burroughs used this method in his best-known book, *Naked Lunch*.

Other notable Beat writers were the poets Gregory Corso and Peter Orlovsky. Orlovsky's work had a natural tone, like actual American speech. Corso's poems were more stylized or formal. Corso even used his writing to create images. For instance, his poem "Bomb," when typed on the page, formed the shape of a nuclear bomb's mushroom cloud.

Later that year, Kerouac hit a new low. He was arrested and thrown in jail overnight for urinating in public while he was drunk.

In January 1965, Kerouac quarreled with Ginsberg. By then Ginsberg was part of a growing countercultural movement whose members were commonly called hippies. While hippie culture had roots in the Beats' antimainstream attitudes, hippies were much more involved in political protests. They openly criticized the U.S. government, big businesses, and other long-standing establishments. Kerouac's politics, in contrast, had grown more conservative as he aged, bringing him closer to the mainstream that he had once rejected. While many hippies piled into cars and vans for cross-country trips—inspired, in part, by Kerouac's travels—Kerouac felt little connection to the hippie movement. Ginsberg's participation in hippie rallies and protests became a source of tension between the old friends.

Desolation Angels was published in May 1965. Again, most reviews were negative, and some were scathing. Critics used terms such as *self-indulgent, rambling, overly sentimental,* and *immature* to describe Kerouac's work.

That summer, fleeing his failures in the United States, Kerouac traveled to France with plans to research his ancestry. He especially enjoyed seeing the country's grand Catholic churches. Although he remained drawn to Buddhist ideas, he still thought of himself as a Catholic. As he got older, he felt closer than ever to the faith, praying more often and sometimes going to church.

But Kerouac was lonely in France, and waves of paranoia sometimes washed over him. He came home sooner than planned. Still, he felt that on the journey he had experienced satori, a Buddhist term meaning "enlightenment" or "awakening." He wrote of this experience in a book called *Satori in Paris*. But the work—published in pieces in the *Evergreen Review* and later in book form—was somewhat confusing and disjointed.

DEFEATED

With Caroline gone, there was no reason for the Kerouacs to stay in Florida. In May 1966, they moved to Hyannis, a small Massachusetts town. That summer Kerouac kept plugging away at *Vanity of Duluoz*. But autumn brought a terrifying turn of events. On September 9, Mémêre had a stroke. It left her partially paralyzed. Bills for her medical treatment piled up quickly.

Kerouac had earlier scheduled a promotional tour in Italy for *Big Sur*. Although he was reluctant to leave Mémêre while she recovered, he needed the money. But his heavy drinking turned the trip into a blur of humiliation, paranoia, and misery. He was too intoxicated to do most of his scheduled interviews properly. His translator remembered one horrible moment: "He was there on the stage under a flood of spotlights, very sad, very desperate, defeated, completely defeated."

When he returned from Italy, Kerouac knew he could never care for his mother alone. So he asked an old acquaintance, Stella Sampas, to marry him. She was the sister of his childhood friend Sebastian Sampas, and the two had known each other for decades. In fact, Stella had long been attracted to Kerouac. She said yes, and in mid-November they were married.

In January 1967, Kerouac, Stella, and Mémêre moved to Lowell together, sharing a house in their old hometown. Stella was an exceptional nurse to Mémêre, and she also wanted to care for her new husband. To slow his drinking, she tried to prevent him from going to bars. But she couldn't stop Kerouac's long fall into darkness, which had been in motion for years. Once a handsome man with shining eyes and a thousand ideas, he had become an unwashed, rumpled alcoholic who spent most of his time drunk, watching old movies on television, or ranting madly to himself in bars. He reeled between moods. Sometimes he wept, and sometimes he danced. He went from shouting angrily at strangers to showing tender affection to his friends. He was so lonely that he racked up hundreds of dollars in phone bills, calling anyone who would let him talk for a few hours.

Jan, shown here in 1984, was Kerouac's only child. When she visited him in 1967, he told her she should write a book and use the last name Kerouac. Jan did write two novels, Baby Driver *and* Trainsong. *Another book,* Parrot Fever, *was unfinished at the time of her death in 1996 but has since been published.*

Remarkably, that spring Kerouac did manage to finish *Vanity of Duluoz*, which had already been accepted by a publisher. Another milestone of sorts came in November, when Kerouac's daughter came to see him. Fifteen-year-old Jan was on her way to Mexico with her boyfriend and wanted to visit her father. During the visit, Jan and Jack talked a bit and compared the shape of their hands, which were similar. As Jan left, Kerouac told her that she should write a book and use the last name Kerouac as her own. This gift was one of the only things he ever gave her.

THE FINAL CHAPTERS

On February 5, 1968, Kerouac's phone rang. It was Carolyn Cassady. Neal was dead, she told him. He had been found in a ditch in Mexico. The two men had not been close since the publication of *On the Road*. But deep down, Kerouac still thought of Cassady as a brother. He was devastated, at first refusing to believe that Cassady was really dead.

That same week, as Kerouac reeled from the news of Cassady's death, *Vanity of Duluoz* was published. Later in the spring, Kerouac traveled to Europe with some buddies from Lowell. But the trip was a string of bad nights and worse mornings as Kerouac consumed huge amounts of alcohol. Back home in May, he spent another night in jail for public drunkenness.

Even as he spiraled downward, Kerouac continued to do occasional interviews. In autumn 1968, he agreed to be on William F. Buckley's television show, *Firing Line*, in New York City. Kerouac had already been drinking before the show, and his friends advised him to cancel. He refused to back out. But before heading to the studio, he got so nervous about the taping that he asked Ginsberg to come with him. Ginsberg agreed and took a seat in the audience. Yet on the show, Kerouac spoke harshly against Ginsberg and tried to disassociate himself from his old friend. Ginsberg, always loving and patient toward Kerouac, treated him gently as they left the studio together. "Goodbye, drunken ghost," Ginsberg said sadly.

Soon afterward, Mémêre told her son that a warmer climate would be better for her health. Later that autumn, he, Stella, and Mémêre moved back to Saint Petersburg.

As 1969 began, Kerouac was still working a little. He wrote a short novel called *Pic* and kept a journal. But his health was failing faster than ever. In September, sensing that his body could not endure much longer, Kerouac wrote a new will. He left everything he had to his mother.

On the morning of October 20, Stella found her husband in the bathroom, throwing up blood. She rushed him to the hospital, but it was too late. On October 21, 1969, Kerouac died of internal bleeding, caused by the complications of alcoholism. He was forty-seven years old.

Kerouac's funeral took place in Lowell. The funeral home was packed with people who came to say good-bye, from Ginsberg to Kerouac's first wife, Edie

Allen Ginsberg (center front facing coffin) *and other mourners walk past Kerouac's coffin at his burial on October 24, 1969, at Edson Cemetery in Lowell.*

Parker. On October 24, he was buried in Edson Cemetery, only a few miles from where he was born. After spending years on the road, writing thousands of words, and pursuing a troubled search for love and happiness, Jack Kerouac was at rest.

EPILOGUE

Kerouac's death in 1969 was not the end of his story. In fact, his legend only grew. His book *Pic* was published in 1971, followed by a full-scale release of *Visions of Cody* the next year. And before long, biographies of the departed King of the Beats began flowing.

Kerouac left a deep impact on American life and letters. During one of the country's most restrictive periods, he dared not only to live differently but also to write differently. He became a cultural icon because of his unconventional lifestyle and the almost mythic qualities of his travels. But his experimental writing—particularly his spontaneous prose method—also ensured that he made his mark as a literary figure. Kerouac broadened the boundaries of the American novel. Writing did not have to be formal and rigid, Kerouac showed—it could be free flowing and alive. As the folksinger Bob Dylan put it, "Someone handed me *Mexico City Blues* in St. Paul [Minnesota] in 1959 and it blew my mind. It was the first poetry that spoke my own language."

Dylan also spoke for many when he said, "*On the Road* . . . changed my life." The book struck a powerful chord in American youth of the late 1950s and 1960s. It inspired them to reject their era's prejudices and strict social rules and to live as fully and freely as possible. Decades later, *On the Road* still sold tens of thousands of copies every year. Other artists copied

Jack Kerouac at his typewriter

Kerouac's style or paid tribute to him in music, television, and movies. Previously unpublished works by Kerouac were released after his death. In 2001 the original *On the Road* scroll sold at auction for $2.43 million, and in 2006 famous director Francis Ford Coppola began filming a new movie version of the book.

Jack Kerouac led a conflicted, controversial, and troubled life. He spent years in search of some elusive peace. And the more he searched, it seemed, the more lost he became. He longed for love and happiness but seemed to find only loneliness and disappointment. Even his writing—his most important gift—suffered harsh criticism, and some scholars still question his work's literary value. But without a doubt, Jack Kerouac succeeded in changing the face of American literature, earning his place among "the mad ones, the ones who . . . burn, burn, burn."

SOURCES

7   Jack Kerouac, *On the Road* (New York: Signet, 1970), 5–6.
7   Ibid., 22.
8   Ibid., 5.
9   Ibid., 180.
12 Jack Kerouac, *The Town and the City* (San Diego: Harcourt Brace Jovanovich, 1978), 3.
13 Jack Kerouac, *Visions of Gerard* (New York: Penguin, 1991), 13.
13 Kerouac, *The Town and the City*, 176.
14 Kerouac, *Visions of Gerard*, 2.
14 Ibid., 1.
15 Kerouac, *Doctor Sax*, 5.
15 Jack Kerouac, *Vanity of Duluoz* (New York: Penguin, 1994), 190.
16 Jack Kerouac, *Lonesome Traveler* (New York: Grove Press, 1989), v.
16 Jack Kerouac, *Doctor Sax* (New York: Grove Press, 1987), 54.
17 Kerouac, *Lonesome Traveler*, v.
18 Jack Kerouac, *Maggie Cassidy* (New York: Penguin, 1993), 29–30.
21 Ibid., 165.
21–22 Kerouac, *Vanity of Duluoz*, 32.
23 Jack Kerouac, *Atop an Underwood* (New York: Penguin, 2000), 61.
24–25 Kerouac, *Vanity of Duluoz*, 74.
25 Kerouac, *Atop an Underwood*, 72.
26 Jack Kerouac, *Jack Kerouac: Selected Letters, 1940–1956*, ed. Ann Charters (New York: Penguin Books, 1996), 13.
26 Kerouac, *Vanity of Duluoz*, 93.
27 Kerouac, *Selected Letters, 1940–1956*, 21.
27 Ibid., 22.
28 Ibid., 26.
28 Kerouac, *Vanity of Duluoz*, 126.
29 Kerouac, *Selected Letters, 1940–1956*, 30–31.
29 Kerouac, *Vanity of Duluoz*, 153.

29 Ibid., 154.
29 Gerald Nicosia, *Memory Babe: A Critical Biography of Jack Kerouac* (Berkeley: University of California Press, 1994), 106.
30 Kerouac, *Vanity of Duluoz*, 220.
30 Ibid., 220.
31 Barry Miles, *Jack Kerouac: King of the Beats* (New York: Henry Holt, 1998), 54.
31 Kerouac, *Selected Letters, 1940–1956*, 75.
31 Kerouac, *Vanity of Duluoz*, 194.
34 Kerouac, *Selected Letters, 1940–1956*, 88–89.
36 Ibid., 88.
36 Ibid.
37 Ibid., 100.
38 Jack Kerouac, "San Francisco Scene (The Beat Generation)," *Readings by Jack Kerouac on the Beat Generation* (compact disc, Polygram Records, 1997).
38 Kerouac, *Vanity of Duluoz*, 267.
39 Ibid.
40 Kerouac, *The Town and the City*, 359.
40 Ibid., 365.
40 Barry Gifford and Lawrence Lee, *Jack's Book: An Oral Biography of Jack Kerouac* (New York: Thunder's Mouth Press, 1994), 46.
41 Kerouac, *On the Road*, 6.
41 Ibid., 9.
42 Gifford and Lee, *Jack's Book*, 125.
45 Kerouac, *On the Road*, 12.
46 Ibid.
46 Ibid., 13.
46 Ibid., 16.
48 Ibid., 57.
48 Ibid., 66.
50 Gifford and Lee, *Jack's Book*, 77.
51 Kerouac, *Selected Letters, 1940–1956*, 173.
52 Ibid., 185.
52 Tom Clark, *Jack Kerouac* (San Diego: Harcourt Brace Jovanovich, 1984), 84.
53 Ibid., 86

56 Kerouac, *On the Road*, 250–251.
57 Gifford and Lee, *Jack's Book*, 156.
58 Kerouac, *Selected Letters, 1940–1956*, 242.
59 Gifford and Lee, *Jack's Book*, 158.
59 Ibid., 156
59 Kerouac, *Selected Letters, 1940–1956*, 315.
60 Ibid., 319
61 Jack Kerouac, *Visions of Cody* (New York: Penguin, 1993), 3.
62 Ibid., 4.
65 John Clellon Holmes, "This Is the Beat Generation," *Literary Kicks*, n.d., http://www.litkicks.com/Texts/ThisIsBeatGen.html (June 21, 2006).
67 Julian Guthrie, " 'Road' Author Still Inspires 35 Years Later; Beat Icon Kerouac to Be Celebrated at S.F. Gathering," *San Francisco Chronicle*, October 21, 2004, http://www.sfgate.com/cgi-bin/article.cgi?file=/c/a/2004/10/21/MNGVP9D9OI1.DTL (June 21, 2006).
69 Gifford and Lee, *Jack's Book*, 87.
69 Nicosia, *Memory Babe*, 183.
69 Jack Kerouac, "Essentials of Spontaneous Prose," *Center for Programs in Contemporary Writing, University of Pennsylvania*, n.d., http://www.writing.upenn.edu/~afilreis/88/kerouac-spontaneous.html (June 21, 2006).
69 Jack Kerouac, "Belief and Technique for Modern Prose," *Center for Programs in Contemporary Writing, University of Pennsylvania*, n.d., http://www.writing.upenn.edu/~afilreis/88/kerouac-technique.html (June 21, 2006).
71 Clark, *Jack Kerouac*, 136.
77 Dennis McNally, *Desolate Angel: Jack Kerouac, the Beat Generation, and America* (New York: Random House, 1979), 339.
78 Ibid., 335
78 Jack Kerouac, *Jack Kerouac: Selected Letters, 1957–1969*, ed. Ann Charters (New York: Viking, 1999), 11.
79–80 Gilbert Millstein, "Books of the Times: *On the Road*" *New York Times*, September 5, 1957, http://partners.nytimes.com/books/97/09/07/home/kerouac-roadglowing.html (June 21, 2006).

80   Joyce Johnson, *Minor Characters* (Boston: Houghton
       Mifflin Company, 1983), 185.
80   Ibid.
81   Gifford and Lee, *Jack's Book*, 240.
83   Ibid., 240–241.
83   Ellis Amburn, *Subterranean Kerouac: The Hidden Life of
       Jack Kerouac* (New York: St. Martin's Press, 1998), 282.
91   Clark, *Jack Kerouac*, 201.
95   Miles, *Jack Kerouac: King of the Beats*, 284.
98   McNally, *Desolate Angel*, 338.
100 Wikimedia Foundation, "Jack Kerouac," *Wikipedia*, 2006,
       http://en.wikipedia.org/wiki/Jack_kerouac (June 21,
       2006).
100 Ibid.
101 Kerouac, *On the Road*, 5–6.

SELECTED BIBLIOGRAPHY

Charters, Ann. *Kerouac: A Biography*. New York: Saint Martin's
     Press, 1994.
Clark, Tom. *Jack Kerouac*. San Diego: Harcourt Brace Jovanovich,
     1984.
Gifford, Barry. *Kerouac's Town*. Berkeley, CA: Creative Arts Book
     Company, 1977.
Gifford, Barry, and Lawrence Lee. *Jack's Book: An Oral Biography of
     Jack Kerouac*. New York: Thunder's Mouth Press, 1994.
Johnson, Joyce. *Minor Characters*. Boston: Houghton Mifflin
     Company, 1983.
Kerouac, Jack. *Atop an Underwood*. New York: Penguin, 2000.
——. *Big Sur*. 1962. Reprint, New York: HarperCollins, 2006.
——. *Book of Dreams*. 1960. Reprint, San Francisco: City Lights
     Books, 2001.
——. *Departed Angels: The Lost Paintings*. New York: Thunder's
     Mouth Press, 2004.

——. *Desolation Angels*. 1965. Reprint, New York: Berkeley Publishing Group, 1995.

——. *The Dharma Bums*. 1958. Reprint, New York: Penguin, 1990.

——. *Doctor Sax*. 1959. Reprint, New York: Grove Press, 1987.

——. *Jack Kerouac: Selected Letters, 1940–1956*. Edited by Ann Charters. New York: Penguin Books, 1996.

——. *Jack Kerouac: Selected Letters, 1957–1969*. Edited by Ann Charters. New York: Penguin Books, 1999.

——. *Lonesome Traveler*. 1960. Reprint, New York: Grove Press, 1989.

——. *Maggie Cassidy*. 1959. Reprint, New York: Penguin, 1993.

——. *Mexico City Blues*. 1959. Reprint, New York: Grove Press, 1990.

——. *Old Angel Midnight*. 1956. Reprint, San Francisco: Grey Fox Press, 2001.

——. *On the Road*. 1957. Reprint, New York: Signet, 1970.

——. *Orpheus Emerged*. New York: ibooks, 2002.

——. *Pomes All Sizes*. San Francisco: City Lights Books, 1992.

——. "San Francisco Scene (The Beat Generation)." *Readings by Jack Kerouac on the Beat Generation*. Compact disc. Polygram Records, 1997.

——. *Some of the Dharma*. New York: Penguin, 1999.

——. *The Subterraneans*. 1958. Reprint, New York: Grove Press, 1989.

——. *The Town and the City*. 1950. Reprint, San Diego: Harcourt Brace Jovanovich, 1978.

——. *Tristessa*. 1960. Reprint, New York: Penguin, 1992.

——. *Vanity of Duluoz*. 1968. Reprint, New York: Penguin, 1994.

——. *Visions of Cody*. 1960. Reprint, New York: Penguin, 1993.

——. *Visions of Gerard*. 1963. Reprint, New York: Penguin, 1991.

——. *The Windblown World: The Journals of Jack Kerouac, 1947–1954*. Edited by Dennis Brinkley. New York: Viking, 2004.

Maher, Paul, Jr., ed. *Empty Phantoms: Interviews and Encounters with Jack Kerouac*. New York: Thunder's Mouth Press, 2005.

McNally, Dennis. *Desolate Angel: Jack Kerouac, the Beat Generation, and America*. New York: Random House, 1979.

Miles, Barry. *Jack Kerouac: King of the Beats*. New York: Henry Holt, 1998.

Nicosia, Gerald. *Memory Babe: A Critical Biography of Jack Kerouac*. Berkeley: University of California Press, 1994.

Turner, Steve. *Jack Kerouac: Angelheaded Hipster*. New York: Viking Penguin, 1996.

WEBSITES

Guthrie, Julian. "'Road' Author Still Inspires 35 Years Later; Beat Icon Kerouac to Be Celebrated at S.F. Gathering." *San Francisco Chronicle*. October 21, 2004. http://www.sfgate.com/cgi-bin/article.cgi?file=/c/a/2004/10/21/MNGVP9D9OI1.DTL (February 20, 2006).

"Jack Kerouac: Bio and Links." *The Beat Museum*. N.d. http://www.beatmuseum.org/kerouac/JackKerouac.html (March 13, 2006).

Jack Kerouac: The Official Website. 2004. http://www.jackkerouac.com/index.php (March 13, 2006).

Lowell National Historical Park. 2002. http://www.nps.gov/lowe/2002/home.htm (March 13, 2006).

Millstein, Gilbert. "Books of the Times: *On the Road*." *New York Times*. September 5, 1957. http://partners.nytimes.com/books/97/09/07/home/kerouac-roadglowing.html (October 12, 2006).

Wikimedia Foundation "Jack Kerouac" *Wikipedia*. 2006. http://en.wikipedia.org//wiki.Jack_Kerouac (June 14, 2006).

FURTHER READING AND WEBSITES

BOOKS

Hamilton, Janice. *Canadians in America*. Minneapolis: Lerner Publications Company, 2006.

Heims, Neil. *Allen Ginsberg*. Philadelphia: Chelsea House Publishers, 2005.

Kherdian, David, ed. *Beat Voices: An Anthology of Beat Poetry.*
New York: Holt, 1995.
McKee, Jenn. *Jack Kerouac.* New York: Chelsea House Publishers,
2004.
Snyder, John. *San Francisco Secrets: Fascinating Facts about the
City by the Bay.* San Francisco: Chronicle Books, 1999.
Worth, Richard. *Jack Kerouac: The Road Is Life.* Berkeley
Heights, NJ: Enslow Publishers, 2006.

WEBSITES

The Beat Page
http://www.rooknet.com/beatpage/index.html
This site offers information on writers from the Beat Generation,
as well as book listings, photographs, and links to other websites.
"Featured Author: Jack Kerouac." *New York Times*
http://www.nytimes.com/books/97/09/07/home/kerouac
.html?_r=1&oref=slogin
This site offers reviews of Jack Kerouac's books and articles
about him that appeared in the *New York Times.*
Kerouac Speaks
http://www-hsc.usc.edu/~gallaher/k_speaks/kerouacspeaks.html
This site offers sound bites of Jack Kerouac reading and
singing his work.

WORKS BY JACK KEROUAC

These works are shown with their original publication dates.

Atop an Underwood. 1999
Beat Generation. 2005
Big Sur. 1962
Book of Blues. 1995
Book of Dreams. 1960
Book of Haikus. 2003
Book of Sketches. 2006
*Departed Angels: The Lost
Paintings.* 2004
Desolation Angels. 1965

The Dharma Bums. 1958
Doctor Sax. 1959
Good Blonde and Others. 1993
Heaven & Other Poems. 1977
Lonesome Traveler. 1960
Maggie Cassidy. 1959
Mexico City Blues. 1959
Old Angel Midnight. 1956
On the Road. 1957
Orpheus Emerged. 2000
Pic. 1971
Pomes All Sizes. 1992
Pull My Daisy. 1961
San Francisco Blues. 1991

Satori in Paris. 1966
Scattered Poems. 1971
*The Scripture of the Golden
    Eternity*. 1960
Some of the Dharma. 1997
The Subterraneans. 1958
The Town and the City. 1950
Trip Trap. (written with Albert
    Saijo and Lew Welch) 1973
Tristessa. 1960
Vanity of Duluoz. 1968
Visions of Cody. 1960
Visions of Gerard. 1963

INDEX

OTHER TITLES FROM LERNER AND BIOGRAPHY®:

Ariel Sharon
Arnold Schwarzenegger
The Beatles
Benito Mussolini
Benjamin Franklin
Billy Graham
Carl Sagan
Che Guevara
Chief Crazy Horse
Colin Powell
Daring Pirate Women
Edgar Allan Poe
Eleanor Roosevelt
Fidel Castro
Frank Gehry
George Lucas
George W. Bush
Gloria Estefan
Hillary Rodham Clinton
Jacques Cousteau
Jane Austen
Joseph Stalin
Latin Sensations
Legends of Dracula
Legends of Santa Claus
Malcolm X

Mao Zedong
Mark Twain
Martha Stewart
Maya Angelou
Napoleon Bonaparte
Nelson Mandela
Osama bin Laden
Pope Benedict XVI
Queen Cleopatra
Queen Elizabeth I
Queen Latifah
Rosie O'Donnell
Saddam Hussein
Stephen Hawking
Thurgood Marshall
Tiger Woods
Tony Blair
Vera Wang
V. I. Lenin
Vladimir Putin
Wilma Rudolph
Winston Churchill
Women in Space
Women of the Wild West
Yasser Arafat

ABOUT THE AUTHOR

Alison Behnke is an author and editor of books for young readers. As an English major, she fell in love with the works of Jack Kerouac, Allen Ginsberg, and their friends. She lives in Rome, Italy.

PHOTO ACKNOWLEDGMENTS

WEBSITES